The Brightness

By Kate Pollard

the big Blake project

Published by The Big Blake Project

49 Aldwick Road,

Bognor Regis

West Sussex

PO22 7BX

www.thebigblakeproject.org.uk

Printed and bound in Great Britain by Impressions, Cambridgeshire

ISBN **978-0-9933385-0-3**

To my family, for believing in me

Recommendations:

"Imagination, pace and character in Kate Pollard's debut novel! Reading The Brightness was like reading the Narnia stories again for the first time. A delightful reading experience...I got lost in the story - what more can you ask? I'm pleased it's now in paperback and plan to have a number of copies on my shelves to give away." (Jane Almond)

"Kate Pollard writes very imaginatively, creating another world where young people have the power to positively affect their lives, those around them and their communities. Kate draws on the power of the imagination as she weaves her plausible tale of light verses darkness, a parallel universe where the craving for personal power comes up against its nemesis. A compelling read."

(Peter Wilks, author of *Jesus - Is How God Sees You*)

"Once I began this story, I found it very hard to put down. The story is highly original, greatly inspirational and utterly intriguing. The short chapters unrelentingly leave you wanting to go further to try to achieve resolution on the numerous threads. But ultimately, even the end of the book only serves to set you up for the sequel! What a compelling read!"

(Simon Day, author of *A Tale of Two CVs*)

"As she was giving birth, one of them put out his hand; so the midwife took a scarlet thread and tied it on his wrist and said, 'This one came out first.' But when he drew back his hand, his brother came out, and she said, 'So this is how you have broken out!' And he was named Perez. Then his brother, who had the scarlet thread on his wrist, came out and he was given the name Zerah."

(Genesis 38:29-30 NIV)

Chapter 1: Awakening

The room was red.

Why had he not noticed before? Xander looked around him, as though for the first time. He saw faces he knew, people he recognised; but did he really belong here? Was this thing that he had become so inextricably wrapped up in the benevolent force that he had believed it to be, or was it drawing him in to something dark and insidious? He knew that this was a pivotal moment, one of defining significance in his life. He stood at the cross roads of time, where the Ancient Ways crossed a sinuous, sulphurous trail and he had to choose.

He did.

He had been fourteen years old when he had joined The Collective. He was mesmerised by Scarlett Tang; they all were. His introduction to her had come through a transmission his school had participated in during a tutorial session. She was young and charismatic. Her beauty had undoubtedly not hindered her cause, but it was not what had initially attracted him; she had ***it.*** On many occasions over the past eighteen months Xander had found himself trying to define what, exactly, ***it*** was. He was at a loss, he had nothing to compare it to. Besides, it soon became irrelevant when she spoke. He didn't care anymore; he was lost – lost in the moment, captivated by her fervour, committed to her vision.

And so it had been, that for the past eighteen months Xander had – like so many young people – entered into a quest that had led him here.

Chapter 2: The Collective

The Collective was her dream. Scarlett Tang had been raised in England by an English mother and a Chinese father. Early on in her life she had sensed the pressing weight of destiny upon her. Her father was a driven, powerful man with high ambitions for Scarlett. He was cold and upright, concerned with duty and honour to a point which she found overbearing. He was a small man – in stature – which he more than made up for in presence; with round glasses set on an almost feline face and slicked back black hair. He was respected among those in his immediate circle, but probably not liked as there was little to endear him in the friendship stakes. In contrast, her mother was quiet, spiritual and deferential. Scarlett did not know if she had always been this way or if it was as a result of years of living in her father's shadow, beaten into submission. She had the opposite effect on people, who liked her (you couldn't fail to, there was nothing offensive in her on any level) but probably did not respect her. Her own daughter found her deference disgusting and she was sure people spoke of her mother behind her back in pitying tones which barely disguised their own acerbity. Scarlett did not feel a particular leaning towards either of her parents or a desire to emulate them. What she did have, however, and from an early age, was the longing for a voice.

She did not have to wait too long. Moving away from home at eighteen to attend university gave her the opportunity she had been looking for to spread her wings and see if she could fly. She was an intelligent young woman, confident and highly motivated – qualities she gained from her Asian parentage – yet reflective and deeply driven by a sense of purpose and identity. She shared her parents' petite and compact frame and her face was open and delicate with large, almond eyes which looked green at times. She had long, raven hair that shone like silk and moved like molten metal. She was arresting and intriguing as a subject to behold and all the more fascinating the more time you spent in her company. So it was little wonder that people followed her as she set about founding a group in her first year of university with the sole aim of discovering whether it was possible to channel the thoughts of individuals into one powerful, collective mind. Scarlett was fascinated by the mind and its latent abilities. She was convinced that it was possible, somehow, to harness the unseen power that resided there and she made it her primary goal to find a way of exploring these possibilities to the point of breakthrough. Initially and unsurprisingly, their success was limited. But with her determination and a small group of committed, like-minded friends, they began to see results.

In the early days they had grandiose and laughably naive ideas about the nature of the group. However, as they progressed and experimented, testing what was possible and discarding that which was mere fancy, they honed their skills. Scarlett possessed a focus and determination which she would later attribute to her father, but this alone would probably not have taken her to where she wanted to go. It was undoubtedly the assistance of a university lecturer who just happened to be simultaneously doing research into mind power, that led to Scarlett's own vision becoming more specific and successful.

She would spend hours - alongside her own coursework studies - with Professor Reinholt. He was of German descent and had worked at various higher education facilities across the world. His work was often scorned by his colleagues – one of the reasons he moved around so much. He was an eccentric individual, whose pyjama bottoms could often be seen descending below the hem line of his trousers. He was the butt of jokes and an enigma around the campus. Many of the students maintained that he slept in his laboratory. But he was a brilliant man who was willing to think outside the box which can be so restrictive, particularly to people of learning. Scarlett liked him.

They had had limited success with experiments on inanimate matter. They would aim powerful thoughts at rocks, both negative and positive. These thoughts would perceptibly alter the vibrations and frequencies emitted by the rock. Encouraged by their work, research progressed to plants. In a relatively short space of time, the plants to which negative thoughts had been channelled became visibly sick and began to die, whereas those which had been subject to only positive thoughts were significantly stronger and more healthy than the control batch, to which nothing had been directed. She saw the damage and sickness which negativity brought about and it alarmed her, but equally she saw how things flourished under love and encouragement and it was this element of the experiment which she chose to focus on. Spurred on by this research, Scarlett became increasingly determined that she wanted to inspire the young people of her generation to join together as one and begin to influence their surroundings – from their schools and home life, to their towns and cities; even their nations. And so it was that The Collective was born.

Chapter 3: Power

Anyone who finds themselves in possession of a radical or original thought, senses the energy that comes with it. The saying, 'With great power comes great responsibility' is not a whimsical notion. Scarlett knew that she was on to something – she felt it intensifying somewhere deep within herself, on some level she could neither articulate or even investigate. She sensed an alignment taking place of galactic proportions which sounded preposterous when spoken out, yet felt true when viewed in the secret place of her own heart. Scarlett was not given to fancy or fantasy and it was this self-knowledge which allowed her to believe she was on the brink of something truly phenomenal. However, she was reluctant to speak to either of her parents about her dream – believing one would crush and the other would try to control the destiny rising up within her.

In spite of her surety concerning the project, Scarlett found that during this embryonic phase she went through a time of relative insecurity, fearing failure or ridicule. Her dreams were dominated by struggles and tension, which she put down to a subconscious battle within her own identity. Seeing this as a stumbling block to the success of her plan, Scarlett decided to use the very visualisation processes and thought control exercises she had learnt with Professor Reinholt, on her own mind. She learnt to focus her thoughts and hone her skills until she felt a white heat of power and clarity. She called this the Glass

Elevator, as when in this state of intense focus she felt as if she ascended in to a high place of power from where she could see whatever problem she faced laid out before her. The solutions and strategies needed to solve the problem would come with such perspicuity as to scare her at first, but ultimately thrill and intoxicate.

"This must be what it feels like to be God," she mused to herself one day, eyes flashing with excitement and exhilaration, after an intense waking vision experience. "I have not stumbled upon this by accident, it is what I was born for." This thought did not intimidate her as it might do with some. On the contrary, it produced a resolve and determination to find a way to develop and share her gift for the maximum benefit of society. It became her driving force.

When she left university at the age of twenty-two, Scarlett worked for a while in the city. Her father was proud – she was fulfilling his hopes for her – her mother was nervous – 'such a big city' – but Scarlett was secretly scornful – they had no idea who she was! It was not about the common markers for success where she was concerned – the job, the house, the car – she was working on something which could do a lot more than fulfil the limited, proud ambitions of a diminutive man from China. She was working on something that had the potential to transform lives, communities, nations even. She did not want to limit its potential to her own thinking – and she certainly didn't want to limit it to theirs. No, let them have their moment of, 'Yes, our daughter Scarlett, she's doing very well for herself. Something in the city, you know!' She smiled to herself. She rarely indulged in a moment of personal pride – she had always hated that characteristic, associating it with a different era – besides, this wasn't about her. Scarlett understood that she was merely the messenger; the one willing to see the vision and make it happen. But she ***had*** seen it, that was the point, and now she was ready to run.

Chapter 4: The Castle

Scarlett worked merely to support herself, but she lived for her plan. Through trial and error she managed to acquire a small team – a couple who had stayed with her from her university days and others, ranging in power and influence, whom she had met through her industry connections then targeted and recruited. But an inordinate amount of work had needed to be done to reach this point.

After perfecting the Elevator, Scarlett worked on providing a place where her team could – in time – convene. She believed that there needed to be a venue in the realm of the imagination which, when given the necessary instructions, people could all find their way to. It was a complex procedure, as she was not working in a physical realm, building something with three dimensional bricks and mortar; she was building something which had no physical structure yet could exist and be visited by others in another dimension. The Elevator had been the easy part, it was as if it wanted to be discovered and used. When she embarked upon it she sensed the movement in her spirit – up, up to a higher plane. It took her to a landscape that at once felt familiar, yet ethereal; welcoming and exciting. She brimmed with enthusiasm and the barely contained, spirit-soaring yearnings of possibility.

Slowly and with the precision and attention to detail of a master craftsman, Scarlett constructed a castle in this new realm of her imagination. She worked on the external appearance of it before inviting a close friend and fellow mind-traveller – Andrea – to come with her and see it for herself. She was anxious that the castle would turn out to only exist in her own mind, but kept her concerns from her friend. Together, after an introduction which involved the use of the Elevator, Scarlett and Andrea entered into a period of rest and focus. To Scarlett's delight – and relief – the results were incredible. Not only did they both ascend together in the Elevator, but they walked around the Castle in union, discussing it in detail. This conversation with Andrea took place in the spiritual plane they had entered but remarkably, she remembered it with great accuracy upon their return. What an exceptional thing this was! She had done it; built something real and alive not just in her own mind, but in the mind of another, and therefore probably another, and another! The stage was set.

With the kind of energy that only success can breed, Scarlett progressed with the intricacies of the Castle before inviting her carefully selected group of fellow adventurers to join her there. They would gather monthly to start with, convening at the Castle to explore the latest room which Scarlett had developed and addressing the particular issues that were governed by that space. It was not necessary for them to be at the same location in a physical sense for them all to be able to meet together at a preordained time in the mind Castle and it was that freedom from the constraints of geography which was the most exciting. The pinnacle of Scarlett's vision was the Throne Room, where each individual in the group had a chair around a circular table. The notion of equality within this group was nominal – all knew that, although they sat around a table with no head, Scarlett was their director. The Castle had been her invention, although they all had access to it in their minds, and she was the one who tended to influence the orientation they took in their thoughts.

It is hard to imagine the power that was growing in this place which only existed in the collective mind of a few individuals. Anyone who knew of it – and in the early days that would be extremely unlikely as in its experimental phase it was highly secretive – would not have believed the phenomenon that was emerging. How was it possible for a group of people in different geographical locations to join together in one place through nothing but the potency of their own minds? How could it be that a place existed in another dimension which could be visited and utilized in order to bring about changes in the natural realm which affected different elements of society? Yet it was so. Within five short years, Scarlett had seen and nurtured something that would ultimately bring a dominance and influence to young people that was previously unrivalled. It came at a time of emptiness, where hopes were limited and dreams unattainable. Where young people were looking for direction; for a leader; for the answer. And so Scarlett stepped up, took the mantle of Saviour of the young and led them into a new era.

Chapter 5: Growth

There is nothing more satisfying than watching the thing you have given life to grow and develop. Scarlett was proud of what she had achieved and the relative ease with which her plan had taken wings and flown. The members of the Inner Circle – as they had begun to call themselves – had become proficient in their skills and what had previously taken dedicated amounts of time to achieve, had now accelerated through practice and skill. This also meant that they could meet more frequently as it was not such a commitment in terms of time. They could take the Glass Elevator within minutes now and be in the Throne Room to oversee decisions and implement strategy.

Scarlett did not have ambition for her own glory – as some might in such a situation – rather, she was single-minded in her pursuit of the Collective. She succeeded in influencing pivotal people in the business world initially, to recognise and financially support what she was doing. She was careful about the people she approached, researching them fully and taking the kind of care one might devote to appointing a guardian for one's children. Her strategy was for financial backing first, then for governmental favour. Within months of having the finances in place, Scarlett had obtained the ear of Peter Nixon, Minister for Education.

With her customary thoroughness, Scarlett had found out that, as a child, Nixon had spent time in a children's home. She admired the fact that he had not had an easy start in life, or the love and support of a family, and yet he had dedicated himself to serving his constituents and to shaping the educational profile of the nation. The Inner Circle gathered together and focused all of their energies on Peter Nixon and impressing upon him the intentions for the Collective. Within days Scarlett received a phone call from Nixon's personal assistant.

Nixon became an advocate for the Collective as a solution to youth unemployment and aimlessness; not to mention improving educational standards. He was excited by the prospects for the Collective and the tremendous transformative potential it possessed. He was soon heavily involved – to the point of taking a chair on the Inner Circle. Scarlett was delighted that he had been so receptive to her ideas and she was beguiled by his charm and enthusiasm. He was a charismatic man; young for a politician. He was ambitious, of that there was no question, but so was Scarlett. He was not someone to stand still, or wait for others to take the lead, but he seemed more than happy to support Scarlett and run with her ideas. He was just what the Collective needed, she thought; someone resolute, obstinate even, and driven; like herself.

Scarlett was careful not to approach too many people. She believed one hundred per cent in her vision, but also wanted to maintain control. With too many people involved in the management level, there was a danger that the plan would either become diluted or it would veer from its course – too many cooks do indeed spoil the broth! She wanted to be the one to influence the direction of the Collective; to drive it and shape it. Her vision was so specific that she feared any deviation from the original blueprint. What Nixon brought with him was the key to the kingdom – a direct green light to deliver her message to every school child in the country if she so wished it. What Scarlett did not realise, however, was that he brought something much more sinister that would insidiously alter her plan and release something dark and disturbing. With hindsight, she may have picked up on a few peculiarities and therefore not trusted him so completely or embraced him so fully. But hindsight is a wonderful thing and betrayal was far from the mind of Scarlett Tang, a pioneering young woman with a social conscience who was desperate to see transformation.

Chapter 6: Early Days

Scarlett launched her plan in a few schools in London initially. It was to be a pilot – although Nixon had already assured her that the programme would go national.

It was the 12th of December, a dreary day that was neither fully winter or residual autumn. Scarlett sat at the desk she had carefully chosen for her office. She was not out to impress anyone, but she felt that her desk was important in terms of what it said about her: too small and she would look like an amateur; too large, she would look vain or desperate. She had gone for a stylish glass and chrome desk, believing it declared her desire to be transparent, yet professional. Her large monitor displayed the Skype link up to five schools in various boroughs of the capital which was imminent. She felt nervous, which surprised her, but excited too. She had been building up to this for such a long time. All of the hard work she had put in, all of the planning, experimenting, trials and reworking had been for this. This moment, in spite of everything, truly felt like the beginning – ground zero. She wanted to inspire the children straight away, to capture their imagination and translate on to them, somehow, her own enthusiasm and intoxicating pull towards the Castle and its possibilities. Over the past few months Scarlett had developed an extensive network of inner rooms in the mind palace, each with its own specific purpose. She intended to show them how easy it was to enter in –

individually or as part of a group – and become one with the Collective.

The intensity of her reflection was interrupted by the entrance of her assistant, Daniel. He was sharp and well connected. He looked like an aftershave advert, she had to admit, but she trusted him completely. She had recruited him a couple of years ago to keep on top of paperwork, meetings, appointments and such. His involvement in the Collective was minimal – a conscious decision as she wanted him to be able to run things from the business perspective, without blurring the lines between that and the main passion of her life. Scarlett took a deep breath, smoothed her hands across her hair and folded them in her lap for a moment. She centred herself and waited, calmly for Daniel's cue. It was like biding one's time, expectantly, for the holiday of a life time, then sitting in the seat on the plane anticipating take off.

"Live in five . . .four . . .three . . .two . . ." Daniel held up the appropriate fingers as he counted down, mouthing the 'one' and pointing at Scarlett when he reached 'zero'.

Scarlett smiled warmly in to the camera mounted on her monitor. "Good morning. My name is Scarlett Tang and I am here today to literally open your mind to new possibilities." There was a flicker of light in her eyes and she moved her hands so her fore arms now rested on the desk in front of her, leaning forward slightly to engage more fully with the camera and the audience that sat beyond.

In his classroom, Xander looked at the large interactive screen on the wall in front of him that showed the projected image of a young, beautiful, slightly Oriental looking woman in a tight fitting red dress. It was as if she was talking directly to him and he forgot about the presence of his class mates. This could be interesting. Better than the usual tripe they tried to inspire them with. There was little introduction to this session, his substitute tutor didn't seem to know much himself. He had been told by the Head of Year to run the Skype program for a motivational session. That was all he wanted to know, frankly. Any lesson he didn't have to plan for – especially this close to Christmas – was a bonus and he wasn't about to look this gift horse in the mouth, so he ran it.

'Another perky little do-gooder!' he thought to himself with a mixture of scepticism and scorn, as he turned to his smart phone and opened the Facebook app. 'These people have no idea about teaching, or the dynamics of the modern classroom. I give her thirty seconds! They'll have her for breakfast!' He smiled to himself and snorted his contempt. For Xander, the opposite effect had been achieved. He put down the pencil he had been doodling with moments ago, in anticipation of another dull session with Mr Glenwood, and gave Scarlett Tang his full and undivided attention.

Chapter 7: The Way In

"I have been developing a technique for harnessing the power of the collective mind. Some of you will hear this and immediately dismiss it as science fantasy; but others of you can already sense a connection with what I am saying. My proposal," Scarlett continued, feeling her confidence rising along with her passion. Her first few words had sounded reedy and thin in her ears, like someone else was talking, but as she proceeded and allowed the nerves to abate and be replaced with the accumulated belief of the nine years investment in this idea, she relaxed and began to recognise her own voice. She couldn't see any individuals on the five small windows in front of her, but she knew in her spirit that connections were being made. "My proposal is that we aim to make a connection which will ultimately strengthen you personally, academically, socially and emotionally. I am deeply concerned for young people today. There is so little to inspire you, yet so much to engage you. You can waste hours, days even, accomplishing nothing. And this is not a criticism of you or your choices, this is an observation of the world you are growing up in. What I would like to see happen through this – experiment, shall we call it? – is that you find something you can both engage with and believe in."

Xander was drawn to this woman. He couldn't explain it, but he had felt the spark of connection she had referred to. What she had – this confidence, belief, drive, what ever you wanted to call it – he wanted it. He shifted forwards a little in his chair with expectancy. He was ready.

"I have developed a mind palace which I call the Castle. It is not a real structure in a physical sense because it only exists on a spiritual plane. Don't be alarmed by this concept, it is nothing to be suspicious of. The whole reason for developing it was so we can have a place where we can meet together through the focus and direction of our minds. In this place, things can be achieved beyond your imagination. The collective mind is a powerful thing and when we join together and harness that power we can literally change the world!" Scarlett paused, she did not want to scare them off with what might be deemed to be, at worst New Age mumbo jumbo, or at best, an over-exuberant idealism, but she felt that a little introduction to the Collective was necessary.

"I don't want to tell you too much about it, I want you to find it for yourselves; experience it for yourselves. Let me start by asking you all to place both of your feet squarely on the floor and sit centrally in your chair. Some basic relaxation techniques can be applied here to get you to a place of calm and focus – that is all you need to enter in to the Castle. Rest your fore arms on the desk in front of you and take a deep breath in through your nose. As you fill your lungs, lift your shoulders and straighten your back. Now release the air silently through your mouth until your lungs feel empty. Close your eyes and repeat twice more."

There were a couple of moments of silence in the room while Scarlett allowed them time to relax. Xander felt a calm come over him and a sharpening of his mind. He felt more focused than he had ever felt before and larger, somehow, as though he had increased in stature.

"Now," Scarlett continued, in a low and seductively gentle voice. "Clear your mind of all distractions and look for a glass elevator. It will take you to the Castle. Do not actively search for it, trying too hard merely prolongs the process, just relax and allow your mind to see it. When you see it, get in and focus on going up to a higher place in your mind. A place of clarity and light. I will meet you there and take you to the Castle."

Xander followed her instructions and found it comparatively easy to visualise the Glass Elevator. He was surprised to see another one of his classmates, Rosie, was approaching it too. They got in and felt it go up. Xander felt empowered, sharp and invigorated as the elevator rose. There was a heat that seemed to exist, but it was more of a colour than a sensation. He enjoyed it, it seemed to touch and wake every cell in his body. The elevator slowed and they got out. He felt the heat increase, this time as a measurable temperature, as did the light. It reminded him of pictures he had seen of the Middle

East; rugged, dusty, hot and bright. He shaded his eyes, looking around. Someone was walking towards them. As he waited, he noticed that a couple more of his peers had made it up (although they weren't in his classes). The elevator doors opened up to release three more young people, but he did not recognise them.

The figure, which had been distorted by a kind of heat haze, suddenly came in to focus; it was her. She stopped a few feet away and smiled at them, a small, slightly awkward bunch of London teenagers. The elevator released two more people in to the brightness of this place he stood in, but did not understand. In spite of the alien feeling of it, Xander was surprised how relaxed he felt, and welcome.

"Join me, please," Scarlett beckoned for them to come closer. "You are the first of many to experience the Collective. Welcome to a new future. Your possibilities have now become limitless; your future is now confined to the boundaries of your own imagination. Allow your senses the freedom to take everything in, familiarise yourself with this place for it holds the key to your future. We will enter in to the Castle shortly and once you know what is in there you will be free to come back at any time and tap in to the Collective Mind."

Xander tried to take it all in, but he couldn't see the Castle to which she referred. He was slightly alarmed in case he didn't have the gift, or the abilities needed to really experience the fullness of whatever this was. He turned to Rosie and whispered, "Can you see a castle?"

"No," she uttered from the corner of her mouth, looking down at the floor. She had a slightly irritated expression on her face which he was unsure whether or not was due to his interruption, or her similar concerns about what they were seeing – or not seeing, as the case may be.

"The Castle is this way," said Scarlett, looking directly at him. Had she heard, he wondered? "Come, let me show you." She turned, looked briefly over her shoulder at the group, then walked back in the direction from which she had come, into the haze.

Chapter 8: Nixon

Although he had not seen it at first, as they walked with Scarlett, suddenly out of the haze, a castle emerged. Made of warm ochre sandstone, it had a high surrounding wall topped with crenellations similar to those he had seen on a family holiday to the Lombardy region of Northern Italy. A sturdy, wooden arched door stood open, leading the way in. Xander felt the assault on all of his senses – the fine, sandy dust under the soles of his shoes; the warm, dry air; the musty smell as they passed in to the slightly cooler air beneath the arch. His eyes adjusted quickly to the light reduction and he saw, across the cobbled courtyard, a large keep. It was taller than the surrounding walls and contained windows – which the outer enclosure did not. They approached the door set in to the wall of the keep and stopped. Although he sensed Scarlett was about to speak to them, Xander could not resist looking about him, open-mouthed with wonder and incredulity. He uttered an involuntary, "Wow!" which Rosie picked up on.

"You're not wrong!" she exclaimed, in low tones. Xander looked at her and smiled. For a moment he had forgotten that others were experiencing this for the first time too. It made it more special, somehow, the shared experience; the mutual admiration for Scarlett's creation. But then she spoke and he felt his attention drawn to her, unflinchingly.

"First, I would like to show you the Throne Room. Who knows," she smiled, encouragingly, "one of you may one day have a seat at the Inner Circle. Although some of them are not present today, as this is not one of our scheduled conclaves, it is where the council for the Collective meet to discuss plans and influence policy." She looked confident, Xander thought, like she was doing a guided tour round a stately home for the hundredth time. This, in turn, settled him. She was remarkably easy to believe in. For a split second he though about how incredible all that he had heard this morning sounded, and yet he had complete faith in this woman whom he didn't even know, and a firm belief that she was to be trusted. As he followed the small group of young people in to the tower, Xander felt a peace and assurance that he was entering in to something of great worth and influence. He felt the privilege of being given this opportunity and as he looked at the almost reverent faces of those around him, he knew they felt the same.

They walked in to the centre of the building, where a narrow circular staircase ran up the spine, with rooms radiating out at intervals – each with a title over its doorway. Xander noticed a few of them as they wound upwards, neatly carved in a Roman font on the lintel above each door – Community; Family; Finances; Relationships. He was intrigued, but pressed on with the conviction that all would be revealed at the appropriate time. His desire to see the focal point of the organisation – the Throne Room itself – increased with every step he took.

Naturally, it was the penthouse, the high place of the Castle. They emerged from the claustrophobic staircase into a large, light room. It was circular, with windows set in the walls giving a panoramic field of vision over the exterior battlements. The light flooding in was natural, yet unnatural at the same time. Bright and tinged with rainbow colours, obscuring any kind of view beyond the walls, giving it the sensation of being up in the clouds somehow. The strangest thing about the room, however, was that the staircase had emerged through the centre of the floor with no kind of banister or hand rail. Looking back at it was like staring in to a large sink hole in the flag stone floor. There was indeed a circular table, but because of the arrangement of the room and position of the staircase, it was quite unlike anything he had ever seen. The table was in the shape of a large ring doughnut with the aperture from which they had emerged at its epicentre. The chairs, evenly spaced around the ring, were stationed on the inner circumference, looking out towards the windows. In fact, Xander observed to himself, each chair seemed directly in line with a window and it was done with such accuracy that it was unlikely to be the result of serendipity.

It was a most unusual sight, and the group stood there in silence for a few moments rotating in wonder on the spot. Without thinking, Xander asked, "Why are the chairs positioned like that, looking out? You can't really see each other."

"That's a good question," Scarlett replied, looking pleased that someone had brought it up. "What's your name?"

"Xander," he replied, feeling a nervous flush rising in his cheeks and the phosphorous spark of connection. He promptly looked down at the floor, feeling not just Scarlett's, but everyone's eyes upon him.

"Well, Xander, it was a conscious choice. It is our minds which make the connection in the Collective. The more we try to see with our eyes, the less effective we are. I feel this gives us the maximum opportunity to focus on the task in hand and not on one another. This is something you will see echoed in the other rooms – although not in the same format. By sitting around the smaller circle, we are also in closer proximity to one another, concentrating the frequency of our collective thought. The windows offer us a focal point where upon we can visualise the thing we are trying to affect. You would be amazed by what we see in them." She smiled at Xander and he felt that spark of electricity again along with a little leap of excitement in his gut. He felt like he was being trusted with something unspeakably powerful and it was new for him – children were usually trusted with nothing, not of any significance, anyway. He liked it.

Suddenly, someone behind him cleared their throat and spoke. "It is good to see you engaging with the programme Xander. We are looking for people like you; people with passion and vision; people who can expand their own thinking to allow for something new. I'm Peter Nixon, Minister for Education. Welcome."

Xander turned as he spoke and found himself face to face with a familiar looking politician. He had seen him on the television when he half paid attention during the hours of seven and eight in the evening, when his dad surfed the news channels. Although there was nothing in his demeanour to suggest he was anything other than the man he projected, Xander – who seemed to possess an uncanny knack for reading people – felt a squirm of unease gripping him, like a cold slug rolling over in his belly. It was not his physical appearance either, for he was every inch the successful city type - a well-cut suit, immaculate hair, toothpaste advert teeth and a Mediterranean tan. No, it wasn't that, it was something in the back of his eyes – a hardness, cold and sharp like the glimpse of a dagger. Xander looked down and noticed the politician had extended his hand. Mechanically, he shook it but felt none of the warmth and encouragement which emanated so readily from Scarlett. For the first time since seeing Scarlett on the screen that morning, Xander felt his defences were on the alert and the cold grip of anxiety toying with him. He looked back at Scarlett. She had seen the concern flit briefly across his countenance and dismissed it – not knowing Xander – as nerves connected to meeting someone who operates in the public eye; or a young boy's insecurity around male authority figures (so many broken homes these days, who knew what the poor lad had to endure behind closed doors.) She smiled at him reassuringly and her eyes, in contrast to Nixon's, were warm and alive. Xander smiled back, relieved and felt his shoulders – which he had not noticed were taught and tense – suddenly relax.

Chapter 9: Rooms with Possibilities

They took the stairs back down so Scarlett could show them some of the other rooms which Xander had noticed the names of on the way up. 'Destiny' was carved into the stone above one door and they all entered it. Unlike the upper room, this was shaped like a quarter of a circle with a single window set into the curved wall. There was nowhere to sit – in fact it contained no furniture of any kind – but inlayed in to the floor tiles in a contrasting stone was a Celtic looking circular pattern. It was a beautiful design which appeared to be made of a single, eternal thread of dark tiles which wound intricately around the room creating what appeared to be four outer chambers and an inner circle. It was a wonderful mixture of simplicity and complexity and Xander admired the construction, marvelling at how Scarlett could have created it. The attention to detail was astounding and he had to remind himself that this place, which to all intents and purposes looked and felt like a Medieval castle built of solid, unforgiving stone, was in fact the figment of her imagination. And yet it was real, it had substance, it existed in all of its beauty and ornamentation.

"These rooms have been developed to provide a focal point for your energies. It is not the rooms themselves which hold the power or the key to your problems, I developed them with individual names to help you to pin point the issues you are faced with so you can come and hopefully meet other mind-travellers with similar needs. That way you can collaborate and support one another. This is the fundamental objective for the Collective, to assist you in joining together and taking control of the things which are important to you so you can influence your environment positively. Before I proceed, I must stress something to you," Scarlett looked earnestly at them and Xander felt the weight of responsibility heavy in the air, "the Collective is about transformation and betterment; it is purely a Utopian concept for the enrichment of society. Any body found to be abusing this facility will be harshly dealt with." There was a pause as the full impact of this statement was felt. Although he had done nothing wrong, Xander felt as though he had just been summoned to the Principal's office.

Suddenly she snapped her head up, the stern expression was replaced by her friendly twinkle and she spoke again. "I want you all to feel welcome, at any time, to enter in to these chambers. I like to refer to them as the Mind Palace and I long to think of you spending time here, enjoying the ambiance and building relationships as well as tackling the issues which touch and motivate you. If you have a specific need, or a desire to affect an area of your own life or society with the positive energies of visualisation, then come; please come and exercise your mind. You will have noticed the labyrinth on the floor," Scarlett continued, indicating towards it with her right hand as she glided, gracefully in to the centre circle. "It is not enough to simply enter the room, you must occupy this central place in order to engage with the techniques I am showing you and be able to make the transaction. If you are alone, simply come and stand here, facing the window." Scarlett gestured towards the aperture as she spoke and they all looked at it. Like the windows in the Throne Room, this one seemed to dance with an ethereal light, as if the spectrum of colours contained within it were alive and mobile. Xander was transfixed, the light was almost hypnotic. It seemed to want to call to him and draw out his innermost desires.

"As you visualise the thing which you are believing for," continued Scarlett, dragging him out of his reverie, "you will find that the colours in the light you see through the window will come together to form an image. They are like radiant but random thoughts which need to be organised by you into something cohesive and visual. That way, you and anyone else who happens to be in the room with you, can focus more specifically on the task in hand. For this reason, it is important that you try to organise your thoughts clearly and precisely as you will achieve the maximum effect under those circumstances. The person in the centre circle drives the vision, any supporters must take their places in the outer chambers. Am I making sense?" Scarlett looked round at the group whose expressions indicated varying states of confusion and bafflement. Nobody spoke.

"Start small, and you will soon get the hang of it. It is simpler than it sounds, I assure you," she laughed. "The Brightness wants to work for you, it wants to become a positive channel between you and your needs. Enough talk, let's try it shall we?" she asked, briskly. "Anyone want to take the floor?"

Xander felt her looking at him, but he had perfected the art of avoiding eye contact in class and refused to let himself be drawn. He had felt the playful enticement of the light, but wanted to see it in action, maybe try it out on his own, not put himself forward as the guinea pig. He heard a movement behind him and looked up to see Rosie stepping in to the centre circle.

"Well done," Scarlett congratulated, genuinely and Xander felt a little stab of regret that he had not put himself forward and been the pioneer of the group. "What's your name?"

"Rosie, Miss," she replied, a little nervously.

"Call me Scarlett, this isn't school Rosie. We are on an equal footing here. Now, we are in 'Destiny'. Is there a small thing that you wish to see accomplished as part of your own destiny? Remember, this is about positive change, so confine your desires to that concept. This isn't about the failure of other people or things, but the success of yourself and what you believe in."

"Well, I have a maths test tomorrow," Rosie replied. "I've always struggled with maths, but I want to get past the mental block that prevents me from grasping certain concepts and excel in it."

"A noble wish. Now, what I want you to do is to focus on the window and relax. Centre your thoughts on the thing which you want to change. Visualise the test if you like and allow your mind to expand and unlock the strategies necessary for your success. Let the reality of it flood your being, grasp hold of it with conviction and believe in it. You will feel it building within you and you will see it projected on the window. This projection is a symbiosis, a mutually beneficial relationship between your mind and the realm of light we are accessing here. Would anyone like to support Rosie in this? There are four chambers, but it is not necessary for them all to be occupied." She looked round encouragingly.

This time, there was no hesitation. Xander stepped up and stood in one of the chambers. Two more were quickly taken by people he did not know.

"Your job is not to drive the visualisation in any way – that is for Rosie alone to do. You need to relax and find the thread of her aspiration and flow in to it. Okay Rosie, centre yourself. Call on your inner strength and the collective mind supporting you here and let yourself explore this."

An atmosphere of calm intensity soon pervaded the room and as Rosie relaxed in to the task at hand the rainbow haze at the window began to show perceptible signs of movement. Before long, the individual molecules of light had transformed themselves from a random collection of hazy hues to what looked like a rudimentary test paper on a desk which contained equations and numerical sequences. With time, these became sharper, taking on a three dimensional high definition quality which was captivating. Then, as if alive, the numbers arranged themselves in to problems, to which solutions equally quickly appeared. A few murmurs from the room broke Rosie's concentration and the luminescent colours retreated back to their previous state. Rosie opened her eyes. She was breathing more heavily and her cheeks were florid.

"Wow! That was amazing!" she breathed. "I know things . . . . I know that I know things now that I didn't know before! This is . . . . Wow! Thank you!" She was at a loss to explain or comprehend the magnitude of what had just taken place.

"No need to thank me Rosie, you did it all yourself." But Scarlett looked pleased by her reaction, nevertheless.

They spent another hour exploring the rooms and experimenting with the techniques, like toddlers learning to walk. The excitement was palpable and the opportunities presenting themselves appeared to be limitless. Scarlett was delighted with the launch, it surpassed her wildest dreams. She basked in the knowledge that she had done something truly great with earth shattering consequences. Nixon hung back, observing from the shadows. In a little while he would introduce his own agenda to the plan. He smiled to himself. This was going to work.

Chapter 10: Back in Reality

Xander was suddenly aware of the low hum of voices around him and the sterile light common in municipal buildings; he was back at his desk in his classroom. He looked around, feeling momentarily disorientated. It was strange that after such a brief experience in the Castle, where he now was felt alien and unreal and the realm he had just left was where he wanted to exist. Most of the class were chatting to each other – except for Rosie, he noticed, she looked as bewildered as he felt. He tried to catch her eye, but she was still struggling to orientate herself.

"Hey, Xander," said his friend, Jack. "What was that all about, eh? Biggest con out! I think I fell asleep!" There was a ripple of laughter from those around him, all of whom looked equally discontented with the whole experience. Xander looked up at the interactive screen; it was blank. For a brief moment, he wondered if he too had been asleep and dreamt the whole thing. To be perfectly honest, the events which had just taken place did seem to be beyond belief. He smiled at Jack half-heartedly.

"Yeah, I know what you mean! Did you see anything?" He tried to ask the question as nonchalantly as possible.

Jack looked at him suspiciously. "No . . . " he said slowly, "Did you?"

"Course not," Xander laughed, a little unnaturally. It was not enough to convince Jack, who was staring at him assiduously, hoping he would give something away.

"She was a nutter!" someone else called out. "Easy on the eye, but mad as a box of frogs!" Again, laughter erupted around the room.

" 'Ooooh, let me harness your mind! I believe in you and I want to experiment on your brain. Don't worry, it won't hurt a bit!'" another person mimicked, theatrically, from across the room, in a loud, high-pitched voice.

"She'd be lucky to find yours, Robbo. And if she did, she wouldn't get anything for it!"

"I dunno, it's probably a genetic throw back. They won't have seen anything like it since the Stone Age!" Everyone laughed, Rob looked a little embarrassed, but shared in the joke anyway. Xander felt uncomfortable. He couldn't wait to leave the room and think things through. At some point he would need to talk to Rosie, see if her experiences were similar to his.

Eventually the bell rang for break. Xander grabbed his stuff and headed for the stair well outside the drama theatre, with his head down. He often went there to be alone.

"Xander, wait!" It was Rosie, he knew it was her. He shoved his way through the door, ignoring her call.

"Not yet," he thought to himself. "I'm not ready to talk about this yet."

Chapter 11: What Just Happened in There?

The rest of the day was a blur, Xander had no idea what classes he had taken. He couldn't wait to get home. Usually he enjoyed school and was happy enough to be there, but today it felt oppressive and claustrophobic. His collar seemed determined to strangle him.

"Xander, wait up!" It was Rosie. She was persistent, he'd give her that.

"What? I have to get home," he replied, tersely. He regretted how harsh he sounded immediately, but he didn't quite know how to deal with his feelings concerning what had taken place during their tutorial.

"You know what! What do you think I'm here for? For goodness sake Xander, this isn't just about you, you know!" She sounded pretty desperate, close to tears even, and he felt like a jerk. "What happened in there this morning?" she challenged, her voice cracking, just as he slowed his pace and turned to face her. He stopped, but he had nothing to say. He shrugged his shoulders, at a loss and looked searchingly in to her face, hoping to see something there to reassure him. She was equally unsettled, he could tell.

"Please. I need to hear from you what happened. I need to know, Xander, please!" Her eyes begged him as her bottom lip quivered, ever so slightly. She was beautiful. Chestnut hair, long and glossy – maybe a hint of colour in it, but naturally done. Her large eyes seemed to be flecked with a range of hues from brown to green and her face was open and friendly, normally so ready to laugh but at this moment pale and drawn. He liked her. Not like that! He just liked her, she was fun to be around and she got his jokes. But he had never seen this side of her and it made him feel anxious and uncertain.

"Okay, you're right. We need to talk. You want to come back to mine? No one's home yet, it'll be more private."

She hesitated for a moment then nodded her agreement. She fell in step with him, simultaneously whipping out her phone and sending a brief message – to her mum, he assumed – as they walked on in silence.

"You okay with that?" he eventually enquired.

"Yeah, my mum's cool. Told her I'm going to the library with Ella to finish my English homework."

That was their only conversation over the next seven or eight minutes that it took to reach Xander's home, a terraced 1930s property on a quiet street in the borough of London they resided in. Each was lost in their own thoughts.

"This is me," he informed Rosie, as they turned up the path to the front door. There was a low brick wall with a gate in it and the short path was tiled in black, white and red rather than paved. Letting the door bang loudly behind them, Xander dumped his bag in the hall and made his way instinctively to the kitchen where he performed the ritual cupboard opening to access two tall glasses and a half empty bottle of squash.

"Lemon okay?" he asked, without looking up.

"Yeah, fine thanks."

With their drinks in hand and a plastic container with some kind of homemade, chocolaty cake in it, they retraced their steps down the hallway to the front room. It was pleasantly decorated in a fairly contemporary style, light and airy with wooden floors and muted colours on the walls and furnishings. They each sat down on one of the two soft fabric sofas which were perpendicular to one another – one facing the original feature fireplace, and the other, the bay sash window. Although it was her first visit here, Rosie made herself instantly at home, drew up her legs and nursed her drink in both hands. She declined the cake – which was also (unusually) untouched by Xander.

"D'you want to start, or shall I?" she questioned, quietly.

Go for it," Xander urged.

Rosie went on to describe the events of the morning as accurately and concisely as she could. To his relief, the order and format exactly matched his own experience. He had half feared that she would have her own account to which he would not be able to relate. He had almost persuaded himself that he had succeeded in dreaming up the events and she had merely featured in his dream on his own terms. He was a little surprised that the infallible similarities of their experiences did not shock him more – surely this outcome was much more alarming in its implications than realising, upon discussion, that they had both had a strange, yet totally unconnected fantasy sensation?

"It was the same for you, right?" she asked, intently. There must have been something in his countenance that allowed her to reach this conclusion.

"It was the same for me," he stated, quietly yet categorically.

"What now?"

"I don't know. I guess there will be some kind of follow up. I got the impression from what was said in class this morning that most people didn't find their way up."

"No. There was no one else there from our class that I could see. I noticed a couple of others from school, but the rest must have come from other schools that were taking part. Did anyone say how many were involved?"

No, I don't think so. I though it was just our class, but it can't have been."

"Are you going to tell anyone?" Rosie asked.

"You're kidding, right?" Xander laughed. "After that reception?"

"Think you'll do it again?"

"In a heartbeat!"

Chapter 12: Algebraic Equations

After a restless night Xander awoke early and lay in bed for a while waiting for the sounds of his parents getting up and ready for work. The excitement and thrill of yesterday's emotional rollercoaster of a day had left him feeling weary and a little flat. There was no time to be self-indulgent, however, as the maths test was due to be held during first period. The test loomed large for many of the students, particularly as it was Friday 13th – although Xander was not superstitious about such things. He got up, taking a little longer to eat his breakfast than usual, partly because he had no appetite or interest in the food but knew it was sensible to start the day with something in his stomach.

He arrived at school just as the bell rang for first period – he would have preferred not to cut it so fine, but it was shaping up to be that kind of day. Besides, the test held no real anxiety for him as he was good at Maths, but looking round the room he could see a few of the students looked less than confident. Rosie was already sat down and appeared calm and focused. Considering maths had always been her Achilles Heel, most people would have been surprised to see her looking so prepared and at ease, but a flash back from yesterday's Destiny Room insinuated itself upon his mind and he smiled to himself. "I wonder," he said, apparently louder than he had intended because Jack turned round to look at him.

"What?" he asked, eloquently.

"Nothing. Talking to myself again," he grinned.

Jack rolled his eyes, "You're weird," he said, as he slung his sports bag on the floor next to his seat.

Mr Rawson cleared his throat at the front of the class and held his index finger aloft. "Settle down Year 10, take your seats. Come on people, we need to get started. Longer it takes you, less time you get on the test. The finish time is a given, remember." Order was achieved more quickly than usual, as Mr Rawson – although an excellent teacher and well liked member of staff – was not renowned for his classroom management skills.

The test was more challenging than Xander had expected, but it didn't really present him with any problems. It did require his full attention though, and was the perfect tool for distracting him from the swarm of incohesive thoughts that had flooded his consciousness since waking that dark morning at silly o'clock. He was surprised just how quickly the lesson flew by and it seemed no time at all before Mr Rawson was calling time on the test and asking them to place their papers – "And make sure it has your name on it, it'll save me a lot of time" – on his desk on their way out. As he was leaving he heard his name and turned.

"Xander!" It was Rosie, she looked exhilarated.

"'sup?"

"I could do it. All of it!" she said, in a low voice, brimming with excitement and confidence. "It really works!"

Before Xander had time to reply, Mrs Jenkins from the Principal's office called them over. "Oh good," she puffed, a little out of breath from the stairs. "I've been looking for you two. Mr Mason would like to see you in his office; now."

The teenagers looked at each other, puzzled. Neither of them was in the habit of frequenting this particular corner of the school.

"What's it about, Miss?" Xander asked.

"I don't know, some project he wants you involved in. Off you go. You are excused from Lesson Two."

They went.

Chapter 13: The Invitation

The Principal's office was in a quieter part of the school, off one of the main corridors with a series of other management rooms. It smelt of floor polish as the linoleum did not receive anything close to the amount of foot traffic of other corridors. There were a couple of posters up on a board next to his room concerning bullying, with a helpline number handwritten on a white strip near the bottom. The door contained a narrow, vertical panel of frosted glass above the handle. Although they could see a red abstract shape through the glass, there was no movement or conversation to be observed or heard. Xander knocked, just below the stainless steel name plate which read: Andrew Mason B.Ed (Hons), and they waited.

Someone stirred in the room. "Come," resonated a deep, monotone voice.

Xander pushed the door open and they were both surprised to see Scarlett Tang herself seated in his office. They had still not met her face to face until this point, Xander reminded himself, but she looked exactly as she had yesterday at the Castle – albeit with a slightly different red outfit.

"So good to meet you in person," she said, beaming at them and extending her hand in welcome. She had risen from her seat and, in spite of a pair of killer red heels, she seemed smaller to Xander – who was hovering at the six foot mark, much to his mother's pride. It was as if the experience at the Castle had put them all on a par in terms of height. Scarlett had mentioned the equal footing there, but he didn't realise she was being literal!

The pair were rather taken aback, it was like meeting a celebrity, but they managed to mumble something by way of a reply.

"I felt a strong connection with you both," she said, animatedly. There was no small talk, she got straight to the point. "What did you think?"

"Er, well, it was awesome, I loved it," Xander replied.

"I've seen the results from our Destiny experience already," Rosie added, desperate to encourage Scarlett.

"That's fantastic Rosie!" Scarlett gave a little clap of her hands with excitement and her smile seemed to get even wider. "I have been talking to Andrew," she proceeded. Xander glanced briefly across at his Principal, just in time to see one of his eyebrows shoot up with disapproval at being addressed in front of a pupil by his Christian name. He smothered a smirk. "He has agreed to let me work with you on the project a couple of afternoons a week after school - after the Christmas holidays may be less of a rush to implement, as there's not much time to organise it now – just so we can see exactly what can be accomplished. What do you say? Is it something you might be interested in?"

"I'm in!" Rosie nodded, emphatically.

"Me too. But why the hold up? Can't we get started sooner?"

This was more than Scarlett had hoped for. "Okay," she laughed. "Meet me in the Family Room at three."

She shook all of their hands again, thanking 'Andrew' very much for his cooperation, and left. Xander looked at Rosie and smiled. He felt butterflies in his stomach and a thrill of excitement. It was going to be a long wait!

Chapter 14: The Family Room

The school day finished at 2:50pm, which did not give Xander and Rosie much time to keep their appointment with Scarlett. Because of this, they decided to stay on campus rather than return to one of their homes together, and they found a room which was an overflow classroom, tucked out of the way where they hoped they would not be disturbed.

It was a grey day and the classroom seemed gloomy and so quiet once the door shut behind them. Neither of them had attempted to return to the Castle since their experiences there the day before and Xander suddenly felt a little apprehensive. What if they couldn't get there on their own? He looked at Rosie. If she harboured the same misgivings as him she did a remarkably good job of hiding it. Another doubt crept in – what if it had just been a one off, like beginner's luck? He could feel the negative thoughts had the potential to paralyse him. It was like seeing a beautiful garden, then being dragged backwards down a dark tunnel away from the place you had such a strong desire to be in.

"Get a grip!" he inwardly accused himself. Then he remembered their meeting with Scarlett that morning; "I felt a strong connection with you both." That was what she had said. She believed in them. The fears subsided, he pushed aside the questions and insecurities and he felt himself regain control of his thinking. Xander steadied himself as he had been taught and took a deep breath.

The sense of freedom was almost instantaneous. Then came the light. Intense light and that sensation again of heat that seemed to be generated inside himself somehow.

Sharp focus and clarity.

The Elevator.

He smiled to himself and got in. Suddenly Rosie was beside him.

"Not thinking of going without me, were you Hot Shot?"

He laughed. "Hot Shot? You're kidding me! Where did that come from?"

She blushed and smiled coyly, "Just trying to lighten the moment!"

It worked. They both relaxed, which had the extraordinary effect of appearing to make the Elevator travel even faster.

"Third floor, haberdashery and ladies' underwear!" Xander quipped, as they stepped out in to the brightness. He had not forgotten the beauty of this realm, but it seemed to make even more of an impression upon him today. He marvelled to himself that he could come here any time he wished.

As they walked towards the Castle, they chatted amiably. "What d'you think she has in mind?"

"Dunno, was wondering that myself," Xander responded. "D'you think there will be others there?"

"Hadn't thought of that," Rosie replied, tilting her head quizzically. "Maybe."

"Kinda hope it's just us though, right?"

"Yeah." And she did.

They entered the keep and proceeded up the staircase to the doorway marked 'Family Room'. It was a copy of the smaller rooms they had been in yesterday and Scarlett already stood in the centre of the labyrinth with her back to them. The window had a picture of a timid looking middle-aged woman in it, but as they entered the room it vanished as Scarlett turned to greet them. She looked a little awkward, as though she had been caught cheating in an exam, which in turn made the pair feel uncomfortable.

"Sorry, didn't mean to interrupt," Xander said quickly, his previous good humour fading. "Shall we wait outside?"

"No! No need. I'm done anyway," she replied briskly, reassuring them with her now trademark smile.

It ***was*** just the three of them, as they had hoped. But suddenly that made them feel rather exposed and a little vulnerable. Were ***they*** the future of the Collective? Scarlett, who always seemed remarkably tuned in to any alteration in emotional wellbeing, noticed their anxiety and her eyes danced. "Shall we get started?" she suggested, with a playful flick of the eyebrows.

Chapter 15: Becoming Personal

"So, let's begin with a little recap. How was the maths test, Rosie?"

Rosie was touched that Scarlett had remembered. "It was good thanks, Miss . . . . I mean, Scarlett. Yeah, amazing. Just have to wait for the results."

"No you don't. You know you aced it!" Scarlett smiled and winked at Rosie.

She grinned back, with added confidence, "You're right, I did!"

"You know this works then, I don't need to convince you. So you'll also know why I believe in it so passionately. I want to see young people taking charge of their destiny and calling for the things they have previously only hoped for. This is the realm where dreams become a reality," her eyes seemed to be charged with electricity and they flashed with her conviction, "where the longed for becomes our every day experience. I don't know how far we can go, if I'm honest, I haven't pushed the boundaries of this yet, but I don't see any limitations – other than those imposed by our own imaginations. You may be wondering why I have turned to you two. Well, you aren't the only ones I'll be working with, there were five schools in the initial pilot phase and I have singled out individuals from that experiment. But I can see that you two are open to the concept of the

Collective and I want kids like you working along side me right from the start. This programme isn't about adults, or even giving adults another way to control children, this is about you guys. This is about giving you the tools, giving you a voice and seeing how far you can go with it." Turning to Xander, she said, "What do you want to see happen, Xander? What's your dream for your family?"

It is amazing what your brain can process in such a short period of time. What takes a measurable amount of time to explain can take an instant to impress itself upon our psyche. Xander was used to operating within his own thinking. He was an only child, so playing and conversing with siblings had not been part of his experience. He was close to his parents, that was not an issue, but he spent a lot of time on his own. He planned, he considered, he reflected, he lived in his head for much of the time. In spite of this, he was a confident boy, able to converse with adults but also popular among his peers. He possessed an unusual level of maturity for someone of his age, but it did not alienate him to Geek status. He was naturally gifted, academically, but proficient in sports too – and it was this which had probably been his saving grace. Other children were willing to overlook his A grade profile if he played on their team, or talked football at break. In that respect he was a lad's lad. Physically, he was tall and broad shouldered – a swimmer's physique, his mum would say, proudly. Ironically, he wasn't much of a swimmer, it was one sport which failed to interest him.

He had the kind of face that made you feel at ease and an even temper. What you saw was what you got, with a kind of effortlessness that made you like him, rather than envy him. He didn't work at it in a desire to be liked, which made it all the more authentic somehow.

His first thought was for his mum. He felt protective towards her, which was silly really, she was a very capable woman. He loved her; liked the fact that he was taller than her and would tease her by ruffling her hair and calling her 'poco mama', meaning 'little mama'- one of the few phrases he had picked up from his father's side of the family. She had not been able to have any more children, in spite of a desire for a large family, and it had brought her so much pain in the early days. But they had found happiness as a unit and he knew that her job as an infant teacher had gone some way to alleviating that yearning in her for another child of her own. As much as he would have loved to make that a reality for her in years gone by, instinctively he knew that ship had sailed; they had moved on.

He turned his attention to his dad. He admired him – a hard-working, quiet man who always put his family first. He didn't enjoy his job, of this Xander had no doubt. He worked in insurance and found the pressure of constantly having to reapply for a position he no longer really wanted was taking its toll. But it is never easy breaking out of the convention of work, particularly when you have a family. Xander knew his dad had a passion for cooking; he was more than a good home cook though, he loved it. What kept him going was planning what he was going to prepare next and ploughing through cookery books and online recipes. These cascading thoughts lasted but a moment and took him to a place where he knew the answer to Scarlett's question.

"I want my dad to open his own restaurant," Xander said, with conviction. "He's good, he can do it. I want him to feel free to take that step."

"Okay then," replied Scarlett, stretching out her inverted, clasped hands in front of her. "Let's do this!"

Xander took the centre circle. He felt a little nervous, he so wanted this to happen for his dad.

"Like this?" he asked rhetorically, placing himself in the centre of the labyrinth and facing the window. He knew what to do, but found that talking masked his anxiety.

"Just relax," Scarlett reassured. "It's not a test to see how well you do, or if you have 'The Gift' or something. Just be real and specific, focus on the detail."

Xander inhaled deeply though his nose and felt his lungs fill, it gave him confidence. He was aware of Scarlett and Rosie taking their positions in two of the other chambers. He looked at the window and took another steadying breath. He thought of his dad and his lips twitched into a smile. The coloured lights in the window danced expectantly, they invited him to make the connection.

"Make this one count," he said to himself. He closed his eyes and the random molecular structure in the window rapidly formed into the image of a strong, handsome man in his forties. He seemed to be looking at his son with pride, as though he knew what Xander was doing.

Suddenly he was wearing chef's whites and working in a stainless steel kitchen. There was a bustle about the place and a couple of waitresses came in and out to deliver orders and collect plates of exquisite looking food. The man looked content, in control, born for this. Then the doors opened through to the restaurant. It was busy, atmospheric, thriving. Customers sat at modern tables eating and talking. The menus bore the name 'Nico's'.

Xander smiled again. "This is for you, Dad. Take it." He opened his eyes and the picture vanished.

"Nico's?" Rosie asked.

"My dad's father's name," Xander explained. "He was Italian and was always urging him to open a place; before he died. It surprised me to see it there, it was like that bit wrote itself. But it makes sense, it's the sort of thing he would do. What happens now,

Scarlett?" Xander turned to his mentor. He felt as if something momentous had just occurred, but simultaneously he felt helpless, like the thing he had just witnessed had moved from this place of safety and security and gone out in to the world by itself. "Is that it? Do I need to keep asking for this?"

"Sometimes things get through straight away, as if they are already lined up in the conduit between this realm and reality, waiting to be received. But there are other times when we do not see instant results. I don't understand the complexities of exactly what occurs here Xander, I have to admit, but sometimes there is more opposition to our visualisations. Be patient though. Your passion to see this happen will drive it forward, so by all means keep coming back to it if you don't see anything immediately." Xander was a little disappointed with this response, Rosie's request had been so instant. But it made him all the more determined. He was going to see a result on this. The Collective ***had*** to work. Already he believed in it more than he ever could have imagined.

Chapter 16: Shocking News

Scarlett had left them shortly after Xander finished his visualisation, she was meeting with another group in one of the other rooms. They were grateful for the time she had spent with them, but not in any great hurry to leave the Castle. They decided not to attempt any more mind travelling, as the experience had left Xander feeling tired. Rosie understood, the previous day had had a similar effect on her. They were content to sit in the courtyard for a while, not discussing anything of any real interest or importance, just soaking up the atmosphere and enjoying their new level of friendship. Eventually, Rosie said she had to go and left him there, his back leaning against the warm, rough stone of the exterior Castle wall. He thought of his dad and what this opportunity would mean to him – to all of them. He felt a pang of sadness as he thought of Nonno, his grandfather, and how much he would have loved to see his son branch out and fulfil not just his heart's desire, but what Nonno called his destiny. Was there such a thing as destiny, he wondered? Was there a path of preference, mapped out for us, or did we bumble through a random series of events which took us from birth to death? This was getting a bit heavy, he shook himself and stood up, stretching out his back and arms. He knew time must be getting on, but he wasn't ready to leave.

Xander was the kind of person who is not content to be told something, he needed to experience it – a trait which had led him to A&E on several occasions in his young life – and that was probably why he was able to function so comfortably in this realm that already felt like home to him. He loved the light, like an Autumn rainbow; the warmth on his skin; the sense of freedom and purpose which existed here. He walked out of the Castle gate and round the external wall to what he thought must be the back of it. He stood looking out from there, but it soon became hazy so he couldn't make out any features beyond. He struck out, with his back to the Castle and walked for quite a while through the barren, rugged landscape, it seemed. Eventually he was aware of a shape in the distance, through the haze and he walked towards it. He smiled to himself as the realisation dawned that it was the Castle that he had somehow come back to. He did not know how he had managed to walk in a circle, but he felt as though it was inevitable, somehow. There was nowhere else to go up here, the Castle was the destination of this realm. Satisfied that he had achieved another level of understanding about this place, he looked for the Elevator and descended, soon finding himself back in the classroom he had entered with Rosie. The gloom had progressed to a vacuous darkness and he glanced down at his watch. It was past five o'clock, his mum would be expecting him home. Xander made for the door, tripping on a chair leg and painfully banging his knee on the corner of a table in his effort to find it. The corridor was also in darkness and he felt a rising panic that he had been locked in for the weekend! He swiftly made his way towards reception, reassured to find lights guiding him like a longed for runway in a storm, to the entrance - which was, to his relief, still open.

"You're here late. Where have you come from?" It was Mr Mason of all people.

Xander wheeled round. Thinking on his feet, he replied, "I've been doing that thing with Miss Tang, Sir." And he left before the Principal had time to question him further, shouting a, "'night. Have a good weekend," over his shoulder.

He checked his phone on the way home. No texts or missed calls, he might just get away with it and be back home before his mum returned from work. It would save having to explain to her where he had been. He was surprised, then, when he entered the house in the usual fashion to find lights on and his mum sat on the sofa with a grim expression on her face. He was expecting a lecture about keeping them informed of his movements, but she hardly seemed to notice him.

"Is everything okay?" Xander asked, concern rising up within him. It was then that the boy noticed his father was in the room as well. "Dad? Is everything okay?" he reiterated. He felt fear grip his stomach, had somebody died? It didn't occur to him to make the connection between his time in the Castle and his dad's early return from the office. He looked from one parent to the other, his mind racing and imagining all kinds of improbable scenarios.

"Give us a minute, son," Dad said, gently. "Nothing for you to worry about, I promise. I just need to talk to your mum for a minute, alright?" He smiled, trying to reassure his son and strode across the room to close the door with a distinct click.

Xander stood outside for a moment in the hall way, looking at the door in a kind of stupor.

"Don't you think you should tell him, Ric?" he heard his mother say, quietly.

"I will . . . ." his father's voice tailed away as he headed for the kitchen. He didn't feel right listening. Was he ill, he wondered? Like his father had been, was that it? The sick feeling that accompanied worry rose up in him, causing a slight tremor to affect his hand as he reached, mechanically for a glass. He put it down on the work surface and stood there for a moment, staring at it, trying to process his thoughts.

"Don't do this to yourself," he scolded and promptly went upstairs in search of his laptop. A little gaming therapy to take his mind off things. They would tell him when they were ready. The glass remained empty, the cupboard door open and a murmur came from the living room. But Xander had escaped for the time being, feeling helpless and a little alone.

Half an hour passed, and Xander heard the living room door open and the clatter of pots and pans in the kitchen. Should he go down yet? He decided against it, focusing instead on completing his level. The smell of frying garlic and onions wafted up the stairs and he felt a pang of hunger. Suddenly, there was a soft knock on his door.

"Yeah, come in," he called, swinging his legs off the bed so he was sitting facing his visitor. It was his mum. She looked like she had been crying.

"Is Dad okay?" he asked, alarmed by how tired she looked.

"He's fine, Darling. He just had a bit of a shock this afternoon. He asked me to tell you – to be honest, I think he's a bit ashamed or something, though he shouldn't be . ."

"Mum – just tell me!" Xander interrupted her, urgently.

"He's been made redundant. His boss called him in mid afternoon and said they had to let him go. He wasn't really happy there, but this came totally out of the blue, there was no office talk of redundancies recently. He'll get a redundancy package, of course, but it's been a real shock for him. He's got to work four week's notice, which, with the Christmas break will take him nearly to the end of January, but . . .

well, that's it really." She tailed off, looking searchingly at her son to gauge his response.

Xander's heart jumped in his chest. "What time was this, Mum?"

"What do you mean, Love?" she looked surprised.

"What time did Dad lose his job?"

"What's that got to do with anything?" she asked, looking puzzled and mildly irritated.

"Please, it's important!" Xander urged.

"I don't know, about half three I think he said. He came straight home afterwards. They let him go early."

"Wow! That's . . ." Xander exclaimed, but trailed off when he saw the look his mother was giving him. " . . .That sucks!" he finally decided upon, with a mock frown.

"Yes, well, who knows what's around the next corner? Stay out of his way for a bit, yeah? Give him some time." She squeezed his knee and got up to go.

"Sure, no worries."

Chapter 17: Man on a Mission

'My Dad lost his job! What the . . .' Xander texted Rosie when his mum left the room. Moments later, there was a soft 'ping'.

'Lol! That's sooo cool! Gonna happen like my test!'

'See ya'

Xander sat on the bed, deep in thought. There was so much to process. He knew he had been given an amazing opportunity and he had a strong conviction that their time in the Castle had directly impacted the decision that had been made by people he had never met, over his father's future in the insurance industry. It was an outrageous notion, but he knew it to be true – he felt it, believed it, could not have believed it more if a troop of dancing penguins had galloped through his room shaking maracas and singing 'This is the truth!' So what now? Most people might at this point be tempted to test out the capabilities of the Collective or consider the possibility of personal gain. But it did not even occur to Xander to go there. Even if he had been tempted, he agreed with what Scarlett said about responsibility. This was not about him or getting his own way, this was a transformative tool. He thought about the ways he could positively affect his school and his community and decided to ride on the momentum of his dad's news.

"I need to make a list," he thought to himself. The organisational side of his personality had kicked in and he reached for the notepad which had a permanent home on his nightstand. He still had on his uniform, so he drew his pen – a black biro with a slightly chewed cap – out of his blazer pocket and wrote three headings as a starting point:

Home School Community

Then underlined each one twice, decisively. Turning his attention to the 'Home' column, he immediately wrote 'Nico's' in his spidery scrawl. It hadn't happened yet, they had only just started on that journey, but he relished the prospect of being able to tick it off at some point – there was nothing quite like the sense of achievement which came when one could indicate the completion of items on a list. There were lists all round his bedroom; on paper, sticky notes attached to his monitor screen, scraps pinned to his notice board. Notes were his thing and they comforted him, somehow, gave him a sense of order and sufficiency.

Xander turned his attention to his mum. He had considered her earlier, back in the Family Room and nothing had sprung to mind. She was happy with life, as far as he could tell. It surprised him, to think of her in this way and realise he didn't actually know what her heart's desire was. How could you live with someone, day in and day out, love someone as he loved his mum and not really know what went on inside them, what drove them? He knew the basics, of course. He knew how she felt about him – fierce, at times, he would call her love. He smiled to himself and felt a little lump in the back of his throat and the hot prickle of tears in his eyes. She was committed to both her 'boys', as she called him and dad, and to their family life. She loved her job, as far as he could tell. But what would be her next step, he thought, in an ideal world? He paused and looked up. His eyes seemed to find a spot to focus on, somewhere on the edge of eternity. 'An ideal world!' How he loved that phrase. How far could this thing go? Was it just going to scratch the surface and make a couple of people's lives a little bit better? Or was it going to go deep down in to the foundations of the nation and fundamentally change it? The prospect of this excited him, although the very thought itself gave him butterflies. He made a mental note to ask his mum, without raising suspicion, as soon as the opportunity presented itself.

Xander felt almost guilty moving on to consider himself, but he did come under the heading 'Home', he decided. He couldn't help thinking about the fact that it was nearly Christmas, and although he tried to turn his back on the sweet image of the latest games console which he had looked at longingly on the internet, it did insist on forcing its way into his consciousness. He was fourteen; he was human! "No!" he admonished, aloud. It takes strength of character to turn away from the things you covet and consider instead the things which have a more altruistic motive. Scarlett had urged him to start small, so Xander thought about the things that he wanted out of life – just as Rosie had wanted to master Maths. Rugby popped into his head. He had always wanted to play for the school team. In spite of being a proficient player, he had continually been overlooked, selected instead for the football team. But it was something he really wanted to do, so he wrote 'Rugby' down in the 'Home' column, saying it aloud as he did so, as if to confirm its place there.

He looked at what he had done so far and thought that his own request could easily belong in the next column. He thought about moving it over, but accepted the fact that there was bound to be a natural overlap as so much of his experience at this time in his life was going to be inextricably linked with school. It seemed the perfect segway to move on to this column and he thought for a while as he gently bit in to the end of his pen. Naturally his deliberations turned to things that affected him personally and it was only a minute before he wrote 'I.T Teacher' in the second column. The department had suffered for a while from a shortage of good teachers and it was time to go on the offensive. His contemplation broadened to include Mrs Berkley, his tutor. She had not been in school for a few weeks and rumour had it that she had been diagnosed with cancer. Was sickness something that he could tackle? It was certainly a big one, but he was surprised to find that, rather than shy away from it out of fear or hopelessness, he felt a gritty determination rise up inside him to give cancer a beating! It had taken the life of his Nonno about a year ago and he hated its insidious nature. "You're going down!" he said, in a low growl of a voice, eyes like flint, and he wrote Mrs Berkley's name in capital letters, pressing hard on to the page with an emotion which went far beyond the concern he felt for her.

Xander stretched his back and breathed out heavily. The final column was trickier. He admitted to himself that he knew very little about what was going on in his local community. Although part of London, the area he lived in had a definite town-ish feel. He got up and went downstairs, calling on his way down, "Mum. Where's the Gazette?"

"What do you want it for?" she asked, appearing in the hall way from the door which led into the kitchen.

"I think one of my friends is in it," he replied. As soon as the lie left his lips, he regretted it. He hated deceiving his parents, but something made him hold back from telling her what it was really all about. He didn't know if she would understand, and he found himself feeling secretly quite protective of the Collective, as though it was his somehow.

"Oh, super. It's in the recycling box. Let me know if you find anything, I'd like to see," she said lightly. As much as he loved her interest in his life and support of everything he did, at times he found it a bit much – and this was one of them.

Xander found the paper and took it upstairs with him so he wouldn't have to look through it with his mum there. He glanced at the front page. Potholes! He could understand people's frustration, but it didn't float his boat as a cause to get his teeth into. Flicking through, slowly, he was on the verge of giving up when he noticed a small column about the local, privately run cinema. The headline read: Rex Set for Final Curtain. He had happy memories of going there as a young child to see various animated films. More recently, he went with his mates to catch the latest blockbuster. It was a quaint old place, with prickly, red velvet seats, a wonky feeling floor and that musty smell that goes with damp, old buildings. It was ornately decorated with gilded plaster and dusty chandeliers. The ticket booth had an old manual cash register and sold sweets like Wine Gums and Malteesers in boxes. The lady who served behind the counter had been there for donkeys years, but still looked the same – thick blue eye shadow and rosy cheeks, something resembling boot polish in her tightly scraped back hair and a burgundy overall with *Rex* embroidered on it in gold.

'Cinema' he wrote, under the third heading. "That'll do for now," he thought, feeling a sense of achievement and capping his pen decisively. He sat back against his pillows, content and reflective.

"Dinner!" Dad shouted up the stairs.

Chapter 18: Dreams and Ambitions

Xander sat down in his usual place at the kitchen table, opposite his mum and with his dad between them on his right. Dinner smelled great – pasta with a chorizo and tomato sauce, salad and warm, crusty bread.

There was an awkward silence to begin with, as if nobody knew where to start the conversation. Normally, it was one of Xander's favourite times of the day – sharing a meal, discussing what they had all been doing that day, but that suddenly didn't feel appropriate.

Mum was the first to speak. "This is delicious, Darling, thank you."

"Yeah, really good, Dad," added Xander, a little too eagerly.

"You're welcome," Dad responded. He put down his fork and finished chewing. "Mum told you, then?"

"Yes, how do you feel about it?" Xander asked, genuinely concerned.

"Well, it was a shock, I'll admit," he replied, "but I think it might just be the best thing that could have happened. I've been thinking while I cooked the tea," he turned to his wife with a gleam of excitement in his eyes, "Dad was always on at me to open a restaurant and there was always a reason not to. Well, there isn't one anymore." He paused before asking, "What do you think?"

"I think this is your time to do what makes you happy, Love," she said, reaching for his hand and squeezing it.

"It will be a big commitment, I realise that, hard work and long hours. But with the redundancy package and a business loan, I'm sure I can get it off the ground." He looked like a young man again, full of hope and vision. Xander was amazed and deeply touched by the transformation, and with a flash of insight he suddenly knew what it had cost his dad, all these years, doing a job he didn't enjoy. At that moment he felt a deep love and respect for him.

"Go for it Dad," Xander said, smiling proudly at his father. "We're behind you on this, aren't we?" He looked across at his mum for affirmation. She smiled and nodded, emotionally. "What about you, Mum? Dad's found his dream, what's yours?"

"I'm sitting with it. You two are my dream."

Xander rolled his eyes. "You know what I mean, I'm serious. What's your deeply held passion?"

She looked a little taken aback by the intensity in his eyes, but decided to answer his question as truthfully as she could. "Well, I love working with the kids. I would like us to start running family workshops during the day and after school. You know, cookery classes, financial advice and debt management, parenting skills, that kind of thing – useful stuff, there's such a gap in this new generation of parents and I want to see them equipped. Only no one has the time to do it and we don't have the funding anyway." She looked both wistful and stymied.

"Would you want to run it? If you did have the funding I mean," Xander asked, trying to sound casual.

"I don't know if I could? I've never done anything on that scale before." She looked unsure of herself and Xander wondered why she lacked the ultimate confidence to step out in to things when she had so much going for her.

"Course you could, Love," Dad reassured her.

"Believe me," Xander said with a strong sense of conviction. "You can do anything you put your mind to."

Chapter 19: Back to the Castle

After dinner Xander returned to his room and updated his list, pleased he now had something to focus on for his mum. He reached for his phone to text Rosie, but thought better of it. He decided what he needed was a bit of time to himself to go and explore more of the Castle – and he was excited by the prospect of testing out the new items on his list.

There was no lock on his bedroom door, so Xander just closed it. He had no idea what his physical body did while his spirit or soul – or whatever it was, he didn't quite know, and until this point, hadn't really considered it – left the place. But he didn't want either of his parents walking in to find him in some sort of weird trance. He had told them that he had homework to do – lie number two – and although it was a Friday night, they seemed to go for it (possibly the events of the day had distracted them sufficiently for them not to question the unusual nature of Xander voluntarily doing homework on a Friday!)

He lay back against his pillows once he had changed out of his uniform and breathed deeply, searching his mind for that focal point that would suddenly burst into the white heat of the Elevator. He achieved it pretty quickly and was relieved to find that it was empty. Upon reaching the realm of the Castle, he disembarked and walked in to the now familiar golden haze that would take him to his destination. There it was, tall and imposing, yet benevolent and inviting. It thrilled him to see it. He quickened his pace, eager to start exploring. Once inside the archway, Xander decided to do a circuit of the courtyard. He had satisfied his curiosity earlier about what else might be up here, but in terms of what other secrets the Castle itself may hold, that was still open to investigation.

The exterior stone wall was uniform all the way around, it seemed to contain no windows or additional doorways. The stones were smooth to the touch and beautifully crafted. The courtyard itself was cobbled, but the crevices between the stones were filled with a rough sand, the same colour as the walls. The sound of his footsteps echoed slightly as they reverberated off the walls. He shook his head with admiration. How had Scarlett done all this? The brief foray took him back to the doorway in the keep – just as the land itself seemed to be all about the Castle; the Castle was all about the keep, no passages or additional rooms to be seen. Satisfied with his investigation, Xander walked in and climbed the spiral stairs with a specific destination in mind. He passed a room named 'Finances' and another called 'Relationships'. As he ascended, he wondered to himself whether or not visualising the same thing in two different rooms where a definite overlap existed would lead to a double hit of power. He decided to test this theory out and retraced his steps to the room marked 'Finances'.

The room was empty, which pleased him as he still felt a little insecure about being observed. He took up the position in the centre of the labyrinth and began, once again, to visualise the restaurant for his dad. He saw money coming in as he focused on the success of the place – money to start it up through a healthy redundancy package and backing and favour for his dad from the bank. There was also money generated by the business itself which would enable him to pay off the debt quickly. Satisfied that he had covered it – even with his limited knowledge of financial management – he broke off from the visualisation and paused slightly before changing his focus and turning to his mum. It pleased him to see her face in the window – he so desired to see her blessed with the fulfilment of her dreams just as much as his dad. He saw her attentively and patiently working with the young children at the school and went on to visualise some serious funding for her community projects.

Xander was encouraged by the intensity of what he had felt on behalf of both of his parents. Scarlett had advised them to be detailed and specific in their visualisations and now he knew why. It was as if the more powerfully you looked for something, the stronger the image was and that, in turn, seemed to pull on the fabric of the cosmos somehow. It was as if the world wanted this reality to exist as much as he did and the Brightness itself was willing it to enter into actuality. It seemed to possess a life of its own and was waiting eagerly for them to come and make a connection. He was confident that something had shifted for his parents and, nodding to himself with a grunt of satisfaction, he left the room and climbed the stairs again. This time he was looking for 'Family', where he aimed to consolidate the thoughts he had just projected towards his mum and dad. On the way, he noticed the room where all this had begun; 'Destiny'. The door was open and Xander saw a man in the centre of the labyrinth with his back to him. A quick glimpse of the window showed, to his surprise, Mr Nixon and what appeared to be people kneeling down around him. Xander found himself pausing for a moment on the stairs and this alteration in rhythm must have broken the concentration of the man in the room. Suddenly, he whipped his head round and glared at Xander. Then, in a flash, he strode across the room and slammed the door. Xander couldn't process what he had seen to start with, and if it hadn't been for the look in the man's eyes he probably would have continued on and not given it another thought. But those eyes; black, soul-deep, what was the word for it? He searched his vocabulary, but could only come up with one that was appropriate . . . . evil.

Chapter 20: Shaken

The shock of that brief encounter broke Xander's concentration and he found himself back in his room without the normal exit procedure. It could have been for this reason that his heart was racing and his palms were sweating, but he genuinely thought not. No, he was scared, he had to admit to himself. He knew, deep down, that he had witnessed something he wasn't supposed to see and that made him uncomfortable. What now? He didn't like that man, he had made his skin crawl right from the very first meeting, there was something about him and now he knew that it was not in his head. The ferocity of Nixon's reaction had given him away and raised Xander's suspicions far more than the image he had seen. It was bizarre, he had to admit, and he had felt something emanating from that room which he had not encountered before in the Castle. Ironically, it was a kind of darkness. What should he do? Tell Scarlett? He shook his head, he couldn't. He didn't know her well enough for a start, nor did he know the extent of her relationship with Nixon. She gave off a completely different vibe, he found it hard to believe she was into whatever it was Xander had caught Nixon doing, but still. No, he resolved, he would do nothing for now, except be on his guard. As tempting as it was to talk to someone, he also decided to keep his suspicions from Rosie. He didn't want to risk getting them both evicted from the programme by throwing around wild accusations about a highly positioned, well respected member of the cabinet –

not to mention, Scarlett's benefactor (or whatever it was he was doing for her.)

"I have an opportunity here," he said to himself, gravely, and with a resolve that he hardly felt. "I can't waste it." It was not his family he was thinking of in that moment, as he uttered those words. It was the hope of his generation, the future for young people that had somehow firmly weighted itself on his young shoulders.

Chapter 21: The Lull

There was only a week left of term before the Christmas break and, in spite of the promise he had made to himself to maintain his involvement in and commitment to the Collective, Xander's experience that Friday evening had left him feeling wary and a little anxious. Rather than raise suspicion and give himself a complete break – which in all seriousness was what he wanted to do – Xander merely scaled down his visits, using the time of year as an excuse which worked to his advantage. On the occasions he did go to the mind realm, he went with and to support Rosie with a couple of issues surrounding her family.

One of the side effects of suddenly finding himself involved in this project and the nature of the issues it brought up for people, meant that Xander had quickly got to know Rosie and found out about some private matters which, under normal circumstances, he would probably never have known. A case in point being that Rosie's mum had unexpectedly discovered she was pregnant in her forties, only to find that it was, in fact, twins she was expecting. Six months ago the two baby boys had been born – one of which seemed much weaker and smaller and had been in and out of hospital ever since with various health scares – and Rosie's parents had consequently been under an inordinate amount of pressure. Rosie feared for their marriage, as their relationship was becoming increasingly fraught from the stress of it all.

Rosie already had two sisters – one twelve and the other nine – so it had been a real shock to consider the prospect of one extra child, let alone two, in a house which seemed to be bursting at the seams already with three rapidly growing girls and all their paraphernalia. They all loved the boys, of course they did, they brought such joy so much of the time, but there were occasions when Rosie yearned for the equilibrium of life before all this happened. She, being the eldest, had had to carry more than a fourteen year old should; but she did it without question.

Consequently, upon discovering the 'Health' room, this was where they had been on the two occasions since Xander's encounter – if you could call it that – with Nixon. Not wanting to arouse suspicion, he focused his attention in the centre of the labyrinth on Mrs Berkley, visualising wholeness for her body and physical wellness. He saw himself pulling a clump of cells out of her body and stamping on them. He was surprised by the direction this visualisation had taken, but put it down to the anger he felt about this disease and the way it robbed people, not just of their lives, but their hope and their peace as well.

Rosie took the centre on behalf of Ryan, the younger and weaker of the twins. Again, this took an interesting turn as Rosie focused on the lights in the window. The string of health issues that Ryan had suffered with in his short life literally presented themselves in the window as a linked up series of conditions – like some form of malevolent bunting – and Rosie seemed to take a pair of scissors to it and literally cut it off so it could no longer connect itself to her brother. The latest tests he was undergoing were for cystic fibrosis, and this was the link in the chain that Rosie had severed.

"What did you make of that?" Xander asked her, as they walked out into the warm glow of the courtyard.

"I felt empowered," she admitted. "But it was more than that, I don't know how to explain it." She looked searchingly at Xander, hoping to find the answer with him.

"It's as if the Brightness wants to help us," he said. Then he looked down, feeling a little foolish.

"That's right," she reassured him, "don't stop. Help me make sense of it." There was a softness in her eyes which both implored and encouraged him.

"I don't know really," he faltered. "I just feel as if we aren't in control of this. We are part of something bigger, cooperating with it, or it with us, I don't really know which way round it is. I just feel as though an agreement is taking place and the Brightness is desperate to show us things we may not have considered for ourselves. To lead us in to a place where these things we are asking for can and will be achieved."

"It is a good thing, though, isn't it Xander?" She looked like a little girl and his heart went out to her.

"How can it not be, Rosie?" he replied, gently, smiling at her and hoping to communicate this fact with more assurance than he felt himself. "Look at what we are doing here? We are trying to make a difference, we are trying to make other people's lives better. How can that be wrong?"

The truth was, Xander did believe what he was telling her and he could see in her eyes that she believed it too. The Collective was a good thing; Scarlett was a good person; what he didn't know yet was whether everyone was on the same page.

During the holidays, Xander was quite relieved to take a break from everything he associated with school and the Collective. It had become intense and enigmatic, so it was good to relax and enjoy family life. He thought about it briefly when his dad came home with news of an extremely generous redundancy package – more than he had dared hope for, he admitted to them both. But apart from that, it was a special time; family time. Looking back on it later, probably the last time Xander had felt that free and happy.

Chapter 22: The Visitation

New Year's Eve had become a bit of a tradition in Xander's house. They had a special meal together, which they all contributed to in some way, then played a board game – something they afterwards said they should do more often, but never did. Then they would head in to Central London to watch the firework display which centred on the London Eye and the Houses of Parliament. It was truly spectacular and the weather was kind this year – crisp and clear but not too cold. They got home about 1am and Xander headed straight up to bed – his parents decided to watch the recording of the firework display first, but he felt so tired he gave it a miss.

He fell into a deep sleep from which he awoke at about 3am, with a start. He had dreamt about Scarlett, but it had been more than a dream somehow. It was as if she had been there in a very vivid, very real way and petitioned him. He could still hear her words ringing in his ears.

"You've been missed, Xander, come back to the Collective. You have a gift for this; we need people like you with a strong moral compass and the ability to connect on behalf of others. I want you to work with me to roll out the programme across the country. I need representatives, spokesmen with whom kids of your age can engage. I need you."

The last words she had spoken, "I need you," were resonating like an echo. He wasn't frightened by what had just occurred, but he did feel the weight of it. He reached up and turned on his bedside light to check the time. He rubbed his eyes, trying to process what had happened, feeling wide awake and alert now. "I need you." He had not been near the Castle for over ten days, which didn't seem that long under the circumstances. But, intuitive as ever, Scarlett must have picked up on his recent reservations. He smiled to himself as he thought that she could have just visualised him back in there, but he knew that she wouldn't do that. She wanted him there because ***he*** wanted to be there; she wanted him to believe in it as much as she did. Perhaps this was his destiny. He took a deep breath, knowing what he had to do. He picked up his phone which lay, charging beside his bed and switched it on.

"You awake?" he texted Rosie.

To his surprise, a message came back almost immediately. "Yeah. Can't sleep. Weird dream :-S"

"Not Scarlett by any chance??!!"

"You too? Might have guessed! What do we do?"

"Only thing we can do. . . Castle"

"See you there! ;-)"

Chapter 23: The Proposal

They rode up in the Elevator together. It never ceased to amaze Xander how beautiful, bright and warm the light was here, and the brief time away seemed to accentuate it. It was perpetual day, filled with hope and expectation.

"Have you been here over the holidays?" he asked Rosie as they walked across the dusty ground. He looked at the way the tiny grains of sand sparkled like granulated sugar underfoot and the little clouds of dust that they kicked up with their feet, showed the full spectrum of rainbow colours which they could see in the windows inside. It was a place to be marvelled at, always bright and new.

"I have, yes, a couple of times. We are still waiting for Ryan's results, but he's been so much better. It could have been an awful Christmas, I wasn't looking forward to it to be honest, but the twins have been sweet; it's been lovely. Is everything alright with you? I thought I might hear from you." She looked at him, trying to gauge his reaction.

"Yeah, fine. It was all a bit full on before Christmas, I just needed a little time."

"Do you think she'll be there? It's a bit of a gamble, it is like half three or something?"

"I kind of got the feeling she wanted us there now. There seemed to be an urgency in her voice. I've never been here at night before, maybe she won't be here."

The determination they had started out with had waned a little by the time they entered the courtyard, but sure enough, Scarlett was there waiting for them.

"Thank you for coming," she said, looking a little relieved. "I wasn't sure if you would get my message. I know it's late – or early, depending on your perspective – but I wanted to start the year as I mean to go on and I was hoping you had the same level of commitment. I haven't seen you much lately," she said, turning to Xander. "Is this still something you want to do?"

Xander was quite taken aback. He didn't realise he was being monitored. He wondered how she knew, but answered quickly, trying to mask his own questions. "I'm fine, it was just family stuff, Christmas, you know how it is."

"I need to see your fortitude and persistence, Xander," she responded, more seriously. "Can you give it?"

"I can." He felt angry with himself that she had had to ask him that question – but he was also a little indignant. She seemed to be coming on a bit heavy, what was her problem? This was voluntary, after all, and here he was in the middle of the night being made to feel like a slacker! He swallowed his pride and looked at the ground.

"Good."

There was silence for a while as they waited for Scarlett to say whatever it was she had called them here to say. Xander glanced up at Rosie, but she was looking at Scarlett, patiently and with anticipation. Scarlett sighed and rubbed her hands against each other, as people do sometimes when they are preparing what they want to say. Sandwiching her hands together, she raised them to her face and rested her index fingers against her lips and just below her nose, her thumbs finding a natural resting place under her chin. There they remained for a few seconds, until she sighed again and lowered them quickly to her sides, smoothing out invisible wrinkles on her red dress as she did so. She sat down on the courtyard cobbles with her back to the doorway of the keep, and they followed her lead, facing her.

"I know it takes time to establish things, I'm not naive, I've been working on the Collective for years. But we made significant progress last year and this year I want it to make its mark. I know your involvement in this is recent and I don't want to overwhelm you with it by coming on too strong. It's just that, well, I've been waiting a long time." She smiled wistfully. "I have been so encouraged watching you kids take hold of this, it surpassed all of my hopes, believe me.

But what it has done, is to spur me on to believing even more in what can be achieved. Peter has said that he will ensure that we get the opportunity to go in to schools right across the country this year, in order to find more people like you who have the ability to connect in to this and thus add to its transformative possibilities. I would like you two to help me develop a strategy we can use to deliver it, which will resonate with your peers. I need your insight in to what works. What do you think?"

"We'll do what we can, won't we Xander?" Rosie answered, looking at him for agreement.

"I'll be honest with you Scarlett," Xander began. "I think what you are doing here is amazing, it's just what kids need – a focus, empowering, something to believe in. I believe in it. I want to be part of this and I want to see it work. But I don't want to be used, manipulated or pressurised in to doing anything I'm not comfortable with."

Rosie was looking at him as though he had just committed a vicious crime. "Xander!"

"No, he's right, Rosie. It's fine. I hear what you're saying and I hope that nothing I have done or said to date has made you feel like that, Xander." She looked genuinely concerned, not defensive or hurt and he felt encouraged by that.

"You haven't, no. I just wanted to make my feelings known, that's all. This is all so new and has happened so quickly. I've just had a little trouble adjusting. Please don't question my commitment though. I will do everything I can to see this become a success, Scarlett. I am all in." And at that moment, Xander knew that the Collective – as long as Scarlett Tang was at the helm – was going to be the prime focus of his life. If, at fourteen years old, you could know what you wanted to do with your life with absolute certainty, then Xander did and he resolved to do whatever it took to give the Collective the best possible chance of succeeding.

"I appreciate your honesty, Xander. Thank you." Suddenly she looked up, over his shoulder, and Xander was aware of footsteps approaching from behind him. He turned his head, just as Rosie had picked up on the same cue and found himself looking at another boy of his age, who he recognised from their first visit to the Castle.

Scarlett stood up, "Oh good, you made it," she said, gesturing over Xander's head for him to join them. "This is Dan, he's from one of our other pilot schools."

Rosie and Xander also stood up, looking at each other with surprise, both a little uncomfortable about the sudden shift in dynamics. Instinctively, Xander stretched out his hand. "Xander. Hi, how'ya doing?"

"Good, thanks." The boy looked nervous and was relieved to be welcomed in. He turned his gaze towards Rosie, who quickly extended her hand, blushing slightly.

"Rosie."

"Hi Rosie, nice to meet you. Which school are you at?" He looked at them both in turn, including Xander in the question with this gesture. Rosie answered for both of them.

"Denman's Academy, with Xander. You?"

"St Philip's."

With the introductions over, they regrouped. "Sorry I'm late," Dan looked a bit uncomfortable, "but I wasn't sure if you were calling an actual meeting right now or not. I ummed and ahhed for a while, then decided to come along and see."

"Glad you did, we've only just started. I'll fill you in on what you might have missed later."

"Are you expecting anyone else?" Xander asked, boldly.

"No, you three are my stars!" she smiled, breezily. "But I expect we will grow as we branch out to more schools."

Xander felt a tug of disappointment at this fact. He liked the exclusivity that such a small group offered, but he knew it made sense. It was nice to think that they were the first wave though, and would be instrumental in developing the programme which would be responsible for helping this thing to grow.

Reseating themselves on the ground - they never actually made it into the tower that day - they spent some time considering strategy and discussing the way forward. It was agreed that Scarlett would approach their Principals – with whom she was already on first name terms – and clear it with them to release the children from a certain amount of lesson time. They felt it would be realistic to start off with spending two hours over a week in the Castle to focus on school related matters – to which it was the school's responsibility to provide them with a list of their requirements. It was also suggested that the four of them would meet on Wednesdays, from lunch time onwards, to first plan their launch, then deliver a rolling programme to other schools around the country. This would radiate out from the capital, methodically taking in more and more schools as it did so. Any time they wanted to spend on personal or wider community matters was to be done in their own time, or through their independent consultation with their own schools.

Feeling satisfied with their progress, the four of them went their separate ways. Dawn was breaking on the first of January, as Xander returned to consciousness in his room. He lay back feeling the warm glow of achievement and was soon fast asleep.

Chapter 24: Renewed Vigour

The prospect of working on the national launch for the Collective inspired Xander and gave him a renewed sense of purpose. He felt that he could concentrate on developing something with Scarlett which would have an impact and reach beyond the boundaries of his life in London. But, instead of causing him to reject his list and the small hopes he had for the people and situations connected with that life, it had the opposite effect and it was with a fresh energy that he confronted the three columns that had inspired him a couple of weeks ago. He realised that the best way to influence people, was to present them with facts. Nothing spoke as loudly as the truth. So if he could get involved in the launch and inspire other young people by being able to recount real events affected by his involvement in the Collective, then the impact could only be increased. For this reason, Xander decided to upgrade his list to a journal, in which he could document his trips to the Castle, the rooms he had visited and the things he had visualised – leaving room to update them (by giving each new event a new page) as and when they achieved fulfilment.

He began by outlining the events which had already occurred.

<u>Dec 12:</u> Destiny Room – Rosie maths test.

(Achieved Grade B on Dec 13)

Dec 13: Family Room – Dad's restaurant

Finances Room – money for Dad/ funding for Mum

(Dad made redundant on Dec 13)

(Excellent redundancy package awarded Dec 23)

Dec 16: Health Room – Rosie's brother Ryan/cystic fibrosis

(Dec 31 Rosie reported he had been better)

Mrs Berkley/cancer

Dec 18: Health Room (as above)

There was nothing to confirm yet whether anything had been achieved where Ryan and Mrs Berkley were concerned, and he had not been into the Castle keep since that day – his last visit had been a logistical one, held in the courtyard, so he didn't include it in the journal. Rooting around in his personal belongings, Xander found his original list. He realised that he had never actually returned to the Family room, as he had planned to do after his time in Finances, due to his encounter with Nixon. As such, he had not had the opportunity to consolidate his visualisations on behalf of his parents to see whether or not a double dose of different rooms added weight to the transformations he was calling for. None of the other items on his list – apart from Mrs Berkley – had been tackled either (and to be fair, he would not have focussed on her if he had not been in the Health room with Rosie; it was more a case of appearances sake than a personal desire to wade in and see her circumstances change. He had not wanted to draw attention to his insecurities at the time.) Xander crossed rugby off his list – as much as he enjoyed it, it now seemed insignificant in the light of his new found drive to see resolution on these other issues.

Over the course of the next five days – the remainder of the Christmas holidays – Xander returned to the Mind Palace on several occasions, both with Rosie and on his own. He wanted to test its limits – if there were any – and tried to work combinations into his strategy as well as spending concerted amounts of time in specific rooms. His family was still high on his agenda and he loved to see the windows reflecting not just his own hopes and desires for his parents, but somehow he felt he could see the Universe itself calling for their identities to be established and their destinies fulfilled. It was truly a special time, which took him to the Family, Destiny and Finance rooms –

for his family – Health and Education - for Mrs Berkley – Community and Finances – for the cinema – and School and Finances – for the IT teacher request. He also visited Health, Family and Destiny with Rosie as they continued to request (although at times it felt like demand, as their confidence grew and their belief in what they were doing proceeded to blossom) a solution to little Ryan's ill health.

On January 15th, an article appeared on page three of the Gazette (the weekly free paper), announcing that the Council had agreed to subsidise the cinema in an effort to keep it open. A large donation had also been given anonymously, to allow for refurbishment – which would commence at the end of the month!

Dad had a meeting with the bank manager, once he had worked out his month's notice (taking Christmas into account, he had left work on the Friday17th January). His business plan was so well received that they agreed to the full amount he had requested for the loan. Xander had to smile when he saw the paper work strewn across the dining table, with the name of the business listed as Nico's. The next step was to find a suitable venue and his dad was currently visiting empty buildings within a five mile radius which were appropriate for a restaurant – either having been used as such already, or being a strong contender for a change of use application. Five miles did not sound like much of a net to be casting out, but in London this offered a host of options and was easily doable. It was important that travelling to and from work did not add too much to what were undoubtedly going to be very long days anyway for his father, particularly in the beginning. Xander took this factor to the Castle too, trying to pin down the location he could see in the window so he could guide his dad – physically with a nudge in the right direction, or supernaturally, by focusing on achieving a certain location on his behalf.

Mrs Berkley, who had apparently been having radiotherapy treatment in the run up to Christmas, was now in remission – much to everyone's surprise and delight. It seemed that no more intervention was necessary – medical or surgical – and she was due back to school on 20th January.

Xander's mum had organised an INSET day for Friday 14th February, just before half term, to discuss plans to expand community and social outreach for the school prior to applying for funding for the next financial year. She seemed to have a new drive and enthusiasm for her job, and a belief in her self and her own abilities which far exceeded anything that Xander was used to seeing in her. He felt no personal pride as he saw the things he had been visualising slowly coming to pass, just the warm glow of satisfaction that comes from knowing that the ones you care about are happy and fulfilled. That their lives have been stretched and their horizons enlarged.

Ryan's tests had all come back negative and he had suddenly started to turn around. He was out of hospital, putting on weight and he no longer needed any medication. He was catching up with his brother in terms of development and the impact on the family had been immense. All of the tension that had surrounded them for the past seven months in which the twins had been with them – and beyond that, the stress of an unexpected pregnancy – seemed to have dissipated as Rosie's parents began to relax and believe that the worst was now behind them.

These personal testimonies were added to his journal and as one item reached full resolution he replaced it with something new to focus on. In the interim, he had also been working with Scarlett, Rosie and Dan on the programme for national outreach. He liked Dan, they hit it off – fortunately – and the dynamics of the relationship he had already established with Rosie evolved to include Dan in a very natural way. They met on other occasions as well as their weekly Wednesday forum with Scarlett, inspiring and encouraging one another.

The Wednesday meetings in Scarlett's office in central London – easily reached by tube – soon became an integral part of their week. She would organise for wraps, smoothies and snacks to be delivered and they would sit on the more informal sofas and discuss their plans for the Collective. Their meeting always started with an update on personal and local matters, which delighted Scarlett and energised the group. They wanted to expand the network, but knew that it had to be done sensitively so as not to either unsettle the delicate balance by flooding it with too many eager young recruits, or lose sight of the core mission statement. This was something they worked on and came up with together and went as follows:

'The Collective is designed purely for the benevolent advancement of individuals and communities and we promise to uphold this in an effort to see transformation for the greater good. Operation hinges on unity between members in order to bring about the Brightness we partner with on the spiritual plane we engage with, and see it released and established here in this natural realm we inhabit. No one is to pursue their own aims or ambitions, particularly at the expense of others.'

Seeing this written down was a proud moment for them all, grounding them in something concrete and consolidating their faith in what they were all so invested in. It was an invitation which they could take with them as they targeted schools in an ever increasing ripple effect from the epicentre of Scarlett's office. They would send out their invitation in advance and recruit new members on a much more selective basis than the original method Scarlett had used of blanketing tutorial groups. With each new member, they were encouraged and with each successful resolution, a deeper conviction was generated. This was no longer a small scale experiment; this was a movement.

Chapter 25: Transformation

Gradually, as the months passed, the small isolated instances which few people noticed, became a crusade affecting whole areas. Xander, Rosie and Dan divided their attentions between their home lives – for all of them things were progressing nicely and they delighted in seeing their loved ones empowered – their schools – which went on to see significant results in the summer exams as well as some excellent appointments of new, vibrant and inspiring members of staff – and their community – which, following the success of the cinema, now had a community action group, keen to preserve the borough's green spaces and buildings of significant historical importance. The crime and vandalism rates had dropped. Recent budget cuts brought on by a national recession had been reversed with the April budget, restoring many services the community thought had been lost for good. Scarlett's office meetings had grown as well, as a small network of new recruits had joined them in extolling the virtues of the Collective via Skype link up (to new groups within an ever expanding list of schools) and through an internet Blog which they all contributed to, and had links to social media sites.

They had initially grabbed the attention of local media, who were keen to establish what was behind the recent community transformations. This had resulted in Scarlett doing an interview for the Gazette in which she talked in vague terms about her work inspiring the young to engage with their community and see it metamorphosised. By November – almost a year since they had embarked on this journey – the national press had got wind of the story and were keen to interview them. It was Scarlett who brought this to their attention.

"I had a call from the Telegraph this morning. They want to run a piece on your school and the changes you have witnessed in your community. This will open up the media floodgates, I'm sure of it, and other offers will follow. Do you want to be involved in the interview, or shall I handle it?" Scarlett asked them, as they sat on the sofas in her office, one steely grey November afternoon.

They all agreed that Scarlett should do this particular interview and, if it did spin off in to more events in the future, they would get involved at that point. There followed a real buzz about the local area, as a couple of press photographers arrived to record crucial elements of the conversion they had all witnessed and to speak to key members of the community about their personal take on things. Scarlett went in to a little more detail about what she had initiated, but still kept the specific details of the Castle a secret. Similarly, although she drew attention to the involvement of certain schools in the original pilot scheme, she did not mention the names of any of the children who had taken part in the Collective.

When the paper was on sale the next day, Xander bought himself a copy and read the article with interest. It was well balanced, describing the Collective as more of an action group than a supernatural gathering. It would be difficult at this point, he agreed with Scarlett, to accurately describe what they were doing with out raising the suspicions of busy bodies who were always on the lookout for a cause to defend. Knowing his parents did not buy the Telegraph, Xander did not imagine the topic would come up at home, but when his mum came back from work she was full of it.

"Hello Darling," she said, reaching up and kissing him on the cheek. "What do you know about this Movement called the Collective? Sandra at work said they have been involved at your school?"

"Yeah, they have, but they are only working with a very small group. Most of the kids haven't got a clue what it's about." He carefully sidestepped the issue, preferring not to lie, but not wanting to tell her the truth either. In fact, the truth was, he hadn't told his parents anything about his involvement in the Collective. It had reached the point now that even if he had wanted to, he wouldn't know how to explain it to them. They had both been so delighted to see their dreams come true – Dad's restaurant had opened in June to rave reviews and was always fully booked on a Friday and Saturday night. Also, his mum had worked so hard on the proposal for their community classes. Funding had been granted and they had rolled out a selection of classes, workshops and drop in sessions from September. Telling them about his part in it would be almost like stealing something away from them. He just couldn't do it.

"Well, I like the sound of it. It's about time kids had something to believe in. I think it's important for them to develop a sense of community and want to affect change. Maybe it's something you could get involved in?"

"I need to focus on my GCSE's, Mum. It's only six months until my exams."

"Perhaps you're right. Think about it though. Besides, it would look good on your C.V."

"Yeah, maybe." Xander left it at that. At least now he had an opening if he ever did need to tell them about his future involvement in the group – they needn't know about what had already come to pass. But it was handy to have a, 'Oh, by the way, Mum. Do you remember that community group you thought I should get involved with? Well I've decided to give it a go!'

Although it was a Thursday, they all got a summons via text message to Scarlett's office again after school.

"Good news!" she declared, with a twinkle in her eye. "We have the publicity I was anticipating. Have any of you been to the Castle to push this along?" It was a bit of an in joke, to accuse each other of 'tampering' if something which they had previously discussed suddenly reached an unexpected resolution. The three of them shook their heads.

"It's okay, I was joking," she laughed. "But, joking aside, I had a call from BBC Breakfast this afternoon. They asked me if I would be willing to nominate a couple of the young people from the Collective to go in tomorrow morning to talk to their anchor on the news show. I immediately thought of you three, I think you could do so much more for the Collective at this point than me. What do you say?"

"For real?" asked Dan.

"Yes, for real! I don't joke about this stuff," Scarlett said with mock frustration.

"You two go, I don't want to," Xander said, much to everyone's surprise.

"Why? You **have** to," Rosie urged, looking incredulous.

"I don't want to, okay!" Xander snapped back, instantly regretting how harsh he sounded, but adamant that he did not want to be pushed on this. He could hardly explain his rather meteoric rise through the ranks of the organization from nothing one day, to one of the founding members the next to his mother. Besides, he wasn't in this to be some kind of poster boy, he preferred the grass roots, behind the scenes, chipping away and watching the transfiguration kind of involvement; that suited him.

Chapter 26: Breakfast

The following morning, Xander turned on the television at the appointed time. Presently, the female anchor made the following statement:

"I have with me two remarkable young people from London. They have been working with Scarlett Tang – you may have seen yesterday's article in the national papers – who has developed a concept called the Collective. Rosie, what can you tell us about it?"

They had gone on to discuss at yesterday's meeting, how far they were willing to elaborate on the intricacies of the Collective and Rosie clearly answered the question, with no hint of nerves, in the manner upon which they had all agreed.

"Well, last December, Scarlett linked up with our school via Skype and introduced us to her invention, which she called the Collective. It is a kind of meditative process, where we unite to focus our minds on positive outcomes for certain people and situations."

"People watching this might think you are involved in some kind of cult. What do you say to that, Dan?"

Dan looked a little taken aback. "Nobody has ever suggested that before, Sally. Scarlett's idea was to motivate and inspire young people to get involved in community and corporate issues. I think you can see, if you read the article in the paper yesterday, that her mission is well on the way to being accomplished. She saw the hopelessness of our generation and wanted to do something to help. I think the word cult could not be further from the truth."

"Well said, Dan," Xander congratulated from his sitting room.

"Tell us, Rosie. How has this 'Collective' helped?" She said 'Collective' as though it was a dirty word and Xander hated her for it.

"Our school has gone from a school needing improvement to one which Ofsted has praised as being outstanding – something very hard to achieve in this day and age, let alone in a matter of months – both in terms of its atmosphere of learning and pastoral care, and in its results, which speak for themselves. Our community has seen a reduction in crime, teenage alcohol related issues, assaults and youth unemployment. We continue to go from strength to strength and it's largely due to Scarlett inspiring us to get involved and rather than accept the status quo, dare to visualise a different future."

Rosie had heightened colour in her cheeks, due to the passion with which she had spoken. But rather than acknowledge that in any way, or give any credence to what she had just described, the anchor changed tack slightly, directing her next question towards Dan. "Dan, I understand you have been working closely with Peter Nixon, Minister for Education. What is his involvement in the project?" Again, that hint of distain. Neither of the children were prepared to be defending their organisation or those involved in it. They had been expecting a pleasant little light hearted breakfast chat about the obvious benefits of the Collective and its glorious future. Xander's anger rose as he watched Sally, the anchor, what was her problem? This wasn't news, it was tantamount to assassination.

Just then, Xander's mum came in to the living room. He quickly turned off the television as if he had been caught watching something he shouldn't. Registering his guilty (desperately trying to pass as nonchalant) look, she asked, "What was that?"

"Just catching the weather. I've got rugby today." The lies came too easily these days and he hated it. But there was a little truth there, he had finally made the rugby team – without any Castle intervention!

Chapter 27: The Throne Room

"Calm down Peter!" Scarlett urged.

"I will not calm down! Who did that woman think she was?" Peter Nixon prowled round the inside of the circle liked a caged tiger. "Making me out to be some kind of zealot!"

"That wasn't what she said. I can see why you are upset, but you have to let it go. She means nothing. No body will remember what she said anyway, the kids were amazing. The Collective itself has not been damaged by this morning's coverage."

"The Collective, no. But she tried to make me look stupid, and nobody gets away with that. She'll pay, believe me!"

"Can we focus on the task in hand please, rather than petty revenge for your wounded ego? I called this meeting so we can build on what the children did today. We have possibilities to call for extra finances, extra favour and a wider platform. Let's put everything in to this and take the Collective up a gear."

Reluctantly, Peter sat down and joined the group of the Inner Circle who were already seated and keen to begin. They visualised an acceleration in financial assistance, an increase in positive media attention and a surge in national support for the Collective.

The energy being generated in the room was exhilarating.

After a while, Nixon spoke. "I've been thinking. I would be more effective for the cause in a more powerful role. Public opinion seems to indicate a lack of faith in the current leadership, which at some point soon could well open up the question of a take over. I would like us to strategise now so that when the time comes, I will be well placed to occupy that position. Will you stand with me to implement that?"

The way in which he worded this speech and the humility with which he delivered it, made it seem a very heart-felt, benevolent gesture on behalf of the cause and some of the group were persuaded to take his standpoint and were on the point of indicating this when Scarlett stepped in.

"This is not about personal gain, Peter. I thought you understood. This is for the children, we are not here to further your political ambitions." Nobody had heard Scarlett speak so vehemently before – she was passionate, yes, but this went beyond passion. It felt, under the circumstances, like an over reaction and many in the group were quite shocked by her rebuttal. "You best serve the Collective in your current role as Education Minister, that is why we approached you in the first place. Do we all agree?" She looked accusingly around the room for support.

"On the contrary, Scarlett. It was I who approached you," Nixon retorted in a low voice.

"Don't be so naïve Peter! Think about it!" Her voice was raised almost to a shout, laced with sarcasm, and her eyes flashed.

The room was uncomfortably quiet as people chose to look at either Peter or Scarlett – or alternatively, at the table in front of them. Scarlett spoke again, more softly and calmly. "I'm sorry, I don't want us to become divided over this issue. I value your contribution here," she looked at Peter, then around the room at the people who had swivelled their chairs round to look at her, "all of you." She paused, "I don't want you to feel you have to take sides over this. We are on schedule with the Plan, let's not get side tracked by irrelevant issues. What we are doing here is a good thing, and you are all vital to its success. We need unity to succeed, we must trust one another and maintain our focus. Yes?" She looked throughout the room at the faces fixed on her, they seemed to relax and many nodded their approval. Scarlett had a gift for taking the emotional temperature and instinctively knowing what to say at just the right time. The potential for conflict was averted and the group looked reassured. Peter bowed his head in deference to Scarlett and held up his hands, as if he were surrendering his stand point and submitting to her greater wisdom. But there was a hardness in the way his jaw was set and a coldness in his eyes. Nobody, in their relief, picked up on it, but this wasn't over for Nixon in spite of all of the body language signals he was giving off to the contrary.

Chapter 28: The Ancient Order

Peter Nixon did not forget things quickly, particularly if he perceived them to be – in any way – a slight upon himself. He had reached his position as Minister for Education because of his sheer pig-headed determination, and because of his involvement in The Order. The Order was a secret, ancient organisation. It was almost mythological to all but its members – those who did believe in its existence, generally also believed that it had ceased to operate decades ago. Nixon got his introduction through a University Professor when he was at Cambridge. The man had seen something in him, a rare but potent mixture of ambition and ruthlessness. Being the man he was, Nixon was interested in the Order in the measure to which the Order could further that ambition. He rose swiftly within its ranks, gradually becoming party to more and more of their secrets. He was not phased by the revelation that The Order was solely created to serve Moloch, the ancient Ammonite god, whose name translated as 'King'. This god demanded sacrifice in return for favour and the greater the sacrifice, the more power you had at your disposal through guides released by Moloch himself. Nixon currently had three guides who he could communicate with and dispatch to do his bidding. They moved in the unseen realm; but their handiwork could be devastating. Like the unfortunate heart attack his predecessor had had, to enable him to pursue his political career.

And so it was with two very specific tasks in mind that Peter Nixon entered the Temple that night to petition Moloch. One was revenge, the other to release the seed of domination that was growing within him.

Chapter 29: A Cloud

"Did you hear about Sally?" Rosie asked Xander as they fell in to step on their way in to school on Monday morning. She looked visibly shocked.

"Sally?" Xander did not immediately register who she was talking about, but he was concerned by her demeanour.

"The Breakfast newsreader. I met her on Friday morning, remember? It was awful. I saw it on the news this morning, she was killed driving in to work at about five."

"That's dreadful! Do they know what happened exactly?"

"They don't give much away, do they, especially this early on. But they said there was nothing suspicious, no other vehicles involved. She seemed to lose control of the car and veered off into a lamp post. Declared dead at the scene, so hopefully she didn't suffer. Can't say I liked her that much, but you'd never wish anything like that on anybody would you? So awful, she wasn't very old really. I hope she didn't have kids or anything – although she didn't strike me as maternal. I suppose it could have been mechanical, or an icy patch or something."

Xander let her talk, knowing it was the shock making her ramble on. It could be a coincidence, but given her recent interview – the rest of which he hadn't actually seen but had heard about from the others – it seemed extremely unlikely that that was all it was. His mind whirred through possibilities, none of which felt very pleasant, as Rosie chatted on, unheard, at his side.

Monday was their scheduled day for going to the Castle to intercede on behalf of the school. It was now a long standing arrangement. They would visit the Principal, collect his prepared list of focus points and head off to a small, quiet room which was often used for one to one pupil sessions, but at this time of the week was given over to them as a meditation room.

As they got off the Elevator, Xander noticed a small, white cloud in the distance. In the eleven months that he had been coming to the Castle, he had never seen anything other than an uninterrupted cerulean sky. Rosie didn't appear to notice it in her slightly agitated state, so he decided to let it go. It was probably nothing.

"What's on the agenda for today?" she asked.

He was glad she was starting to come back from the shock of the morning's news to a point where she was able again to focus on the task in hand. He had wondered, earlier, if it was worth them coming today

– a distracted mind is not the best tool to bring to such a place as the Castle.

"A new maths teacher for January; Mrs Skelton's baby's due any day; the server keeps crashing; and the weather for the cross country competition in Richmond Park," he replied, glancing down at the neatly typed list as they climbed the stairs to 'Education'. They had recently made the discovery that even something as potentially abstract as the weather was still just as pliant as a physical thing. Everything, it seemed, had the capacity to be affected by the Brightness.

As he looked up, Xander caught a brief glimpse of what appeared to be a person in some kind of flowing white garment, disappearing around the curve of the spiral staircase ahead.

"Who was that?" he asked, sceptically.

"Who was what?" She ***was*** still distracted, in spite of his hopes to the contrary.

"Someone just came out of here and went upstairs."

"So? We're not the only ones here, Xander," she snorted, disparagingly.

"I know!" he retorted, unable to keep his frustration with her from his voice. "It's not that. They just seemed a bit odd. I think they were wearing a long white dress or a robe or something."

"Maybe one of the Inner Circle, some of them are a bit 'theatrical'," she used her index fingers to indicate parentheses in the air, and pulled a bit of a face.

Xander nodded, but he couldn't shake a rather unpleasant sensation which had come upon him, that all was not well in the Castle; something had shifted.

Chapter 30: Phase Two

Scarlett Tang may have had a carefully thought out, step by step plan for the unveiling of and implementation of the Collective, but Peter Nixon also had an objective and his had progressed from phase one – in which he remained dormant and supportive within the higher echelons of the Inner Circle until such a time as he could progress to the next phase and introduce his own, slightly different agenda. That time had now arrived. It is true to say that the reaction to Sally Boreman's interview the other day had forced his hand slightly – she couldn't be allowed to get away with it – and so he had escalated his plan more quickly that he would have liked. But he was impatient; there was only so long he was prepared to sit there and take Scarlett's condescending attitude towards him.

He thought of Sally and smiled to himself. He had asked one of his spirit guides to cover her eyes on a particularly sharp bend that lay on her route to work. "Nobody mocks me, lady," he murmured, in a self congratulating fashion.

The second phase was all about infiltration. The deeper he had gone in to The Order, the more he realised the need for an edge – Peter Nixon did nothing without carefully considering his place in it and how he could be seen to supreme advantage. It was always about getting the best he could for himself. His priority now was to raise his own profile over and above those of the other members of The Order, so that Moloch would favour him and he could negotiate his way into a position of power. His decision to gain the post of Minister for Education was not an arbitrary one – it was certainly not about the Collective – it was in order to serve Moloch and ultimately become more powerful, a stepping stone to higher things. In fact, the Collective had been a serendipitous addition to his plan. Scarlett Tang may be thinking that Peter Nixon was serving her cause, but he was about to turn the tables on her – and, oh, the possibilities it opened up were tantalizing!

Formulating his game plan required an understanding of who Moloch was and what he stood for. Nixon had done his research and discovered that Moloch was a god of the Ammonite people from the ancient near east – present day Jordan. According to genealogy, they were the descendants of Lot – who was nephew to Abraham – through his second daughter's son, Ben-Ammi. The Ammonites and the Israelites were at odds for many years and the god Moloch supplanted Jehovah. The people worshipped him and, in order to appease him, they offered child sacrifices in a ceremony of passing through the fire, which was an abomination to Jehovah. But, he was undefeated and remained 'the King' in this London temple, hidden away and all but forgotten. Nixon knew that if he could satisfy Moloch's lust for blood, he would become exceptionally powerful. He was an unusual man, as many serve their gods out of a sense of belonging or to be pleasing to them in some way. Nixon was after the ultimate goal, to be worshipped in his own right and he had the audacity to see Moloch as a means to that end.

He had met Moloch face to face, without fear. He had a calf's head and a man's body, with an imposing stature. His arms were perpetually outstretched to receive the offering of children – which in ancient times had been done, horrifyingly enough, by their parents, under the misapprehension that it would bring them blessing. His plan, which he had discussed with Moloch and gained his approval for, was to captivate the minds of the children of this generation – not as a physical blood sacrifice, but as a servant for the cause. It may be necessary from time to time to take a life, in order to satiate the god's appetite, but it was not necessary for that to always be a youngster – are we not all somebody's child?

The Collective had come along at just the right time, it was a gift! He had bided his time with patience and there it was – the perfect tool for enrolling children without raising suspicion. It was now time to release the guides in to the mind palace to recruit the recruits. He did not share this with his contemporaries at either the Temple or the Collective. No, he wanted this power for himself. He wanted to dominate it, shape it, use it to further his ambitions. After he had dispatched with Sally – satisfying his wounded pride and his master's lust for blood – he went on to release one of his favourite guides in to the Castle. The guide disguised himself as a woman; blonde, alluring, robed in white; and took on the name Naamah – meaning beautiful. Gradually Nixon planned on releasing other guides, but he had to be discrete so as not to be discovered before he had enough in place to ensure the success of his plan.

Naamah had been tasked with installing another doorway in to the Castle walls. This would allow the freedom of movement of the other guides into the Castle, when the time was right. She was inherently merciless, but she hid it well behind a persona carefully crafted for the purpose. Nixon trusted no one, in truth, but he needed Naamah to succeed, and she knew it. She had been anxious to secure her invitation to the Castle – the beings of the unseen realm knew of its existence and the faction Naamah belonged to were uneasy about it. They wanted to get in to the Mind Palace as much as Nixon did; they hated anything with such a pure motive and longed to pollute it. Xander was right, something unquestionably had shifted and there was no going back.

Chapter 31: An Experiment

Naamah was indeed beautiful. She looked like an Athenian princess. Everything about her seemed to shine with light; from her golden hair that had the iridescent opalescence of mother of pearl about it, to her complexion which also seemed to glow with an amber radiance set off by the most beautiful indigo eyes, to her pure white garment that fell about her shapely form like a thousand butterfly wings. But it was all a deception. Beneath that outer shell of beauty was the guide – who Nixon was familiar with – and who, ironically, was a faceless, shrouded figure with no inherent radiant light at all. In fact, he exuded a greyness which seemed to cancel out anything of radiance or beauty that he came in to contact with – as if he sucked the very essence out of things in his sphere of influence. That too was a façade, however, and even Nixon himself had not seen the creature that lurked beneath that disguise. The guides showed people what they expected to see and although Nixon was under no illusion about the realm he was operating within, by its very nature it was fraught with distortions; smoke and mirrors. In his own mind, the guides Nixon saw suited his own purposes and perceptions. They did his bidding – which was his main concern – in an almost invisible silence, hiding their lasciviousness and repulsive appearance well.

The Collective had come along just at the right time for Nixon. He had already obtained the position of

Minister for Education, knowing this would give him a certain amount of favour where Moloch was concerned. Access to children was his desire, but it was not with any depravity that he sought this connection, he merely saw it as a means to feed his master's lust and as such obtain more power. He was at a critical juncture; he had the authority, he merely lacked the access point. That is where Scarlett – unbeknown to her – came in. Now he had a way of manipulating children, through the unity of the collective mind, to serve his own vision. His plan to infiltrate the Collective was foolproof. The beauty of it delighted him beyond words. To be able to invite the children in with the lure of a benevolent and transformative brightness, then distort their path, without their knowledge, so they were channelled in to the shadier realm of Moloch, was sheer ecstasy. His own path in to Moloch's service had been a gradual introduction with ever increasing revelation about who exactly he was following. The children, likewise, would be lured in incrementally – initially through the perfect window of Scarlett's creation, until, little by little, almost imperceptibly if he played it just right, they would be shifted in to a new place, of his creation, where he would rule and Moloch would be satisfied.

Greed is a powerful motivator. It drives people in different ways. It was not about money though, not for Nixon, it was power he craved to the point of omnipotence. He knew that he could ruin everything through impatience or pride – both of which lead, almost without exception, to poor decision making and failure. He could do patience, he wasn't about to blow what he had spent years waiting to achieve. Like any successful predator, he knew that concealment up until the absolute last moment, was the key.

The door he had installed was behind the keep – nobody went round there, particularly these days. Maybe early on a few eager young adventurers had gone on a fact finding mission and explored every inch of the Castle and its surroundings, but the new recruits were all told there was nothing else to see and nobody, it seemed, felt the need to question that fact. It had required intense concentration on Nixon's part and some assistance from his guides to increase the potency of directional thought, to override Scarlett's initial construction. He was impressed by the solidity of this abstract edifice and he had more respect for Scarlett as a consequence. Finally though, the wall had warped and contorted and the doorway that marked the beginning of his dominion appeared. He hoped it was hidden away enough to remain undiscovered – or at the very least, unquestioned – as to see it there brought a flush of insecurity for a moment. But it did not last as the thought of what was now possible took shape in his mind.

He was thorough in his preparations, doing nothing without strategising at least a couple of moves ahead – he would have made an excellent chess player!

Nixon had already selected a child to be his primary target. In true predatory fashion, he looked for a weakness in the herd which seemed to be ever increasing at all times of the day and night. There were obviously periods of more intense activity and he decided to avoid these times to prowl the confines of the Castle in search of potential pawns. Lucie was thirteen years old and quite a shy girl. She was plain looking, indistinct might be a better description, and as such many people failed to even notice her. She seemed to have few friends and most of the time operated on her own or on the periphery. After observing her for some time and finding out as much as he could about her without raising suspicion, Nixon went to the Throne Room one night, alone, and summoned Naamah to visit Lucie in a dream.

It was three o'clock in the morning and Lucie was having the most amazing fantasy. In it, a beautiful woman – no, ***the*** most beautiful woman that Lucie had ever seen - came and sat with her in a garden. It was warm and sunny, with the thick scent of flowers in the air. A bee buzzed lazily by and the sunlight was shimmering with rainbows. The woman spoke to her in a voice as smooth as honey, yet with the delicacy and purity of crystal.

"Lucie, I know you. I have watched you grow up. I have seen your loneliness. You are special, Lucie. You are set apart for great things."

"Who are you?" the dreaming Lucie asked, not the least afraid of the stranger. On the contrary, she was captivated by her.

"I am your guardian, child. Your spiritual mother."

"Do you know my mother?" The words she had uttered got exactly the response that Naamah was hoping for. Lucie's mother had died from a terminal illness when Lucie was six and this had left her vulnerable, desperate for a mother's touch. She had eagerly engaged with the woman through her question.

"Yes, child," she lied, effortlessly. "I know her. She asked me to take care of you." When you have a longing in your heart and someone comes along with the promise of satisfying that longing, it is so easy to trust them without caution. Naamah's words had the ring of truth for Lucie, so her damaged little heart sought out what was being offered to her.

"Can I see her?" The hunger in her voice was palpable.

"She's in the Castle. There is so much yet to be revealed there my dear that you haven't been told about yet. But you have been chosen to lead others in to the rooms of enlightenment. There is a secret door. It will take you to her and open up new possibilities for others like you. Do you want to come?" The apparition in her dream started to fade away, her arms outstretched towards Lucie and her face smiling an invitation.

"Yes! Yes! Mum!" Lucie called out, "Mum, where are you?"

Her father heard her calling out from his room and came quickly to reassure her. Nightmares were not uncommon for his little girl, and each time she called out in the night for her mother it broke his heart.

"Hey, Sweetie. What's up? I'm here."

"Dad? I had a dream . . . ." Lucie stopped herself as she became more conscious and remembered more of the powerful dream she had had.

"It's okay Love. Nothing can hurt you now. Try and get some sleep," he said comfortingly.

"I'm okay, Dad. I promise," she smiled at him as he stroked her hair back from her face. "Thanks." She needed him to leave her. She had to get to the Castle, as soon as possible.

Chapter 32: Behind the Door

As soon as her dad had gone back to bed, Lucie lost no time in visualising herself into the Castle. She ran from the Elevator in to the courtyard – it was deserted, and she stopped abruptly to think about what exactly Naamah had said. Suddenly she was there, materialising from the doorway that led into the keep.

"You came, Lucie," she said, smiling joyfully and offering both her hands to the girl in friendship. It was a warm gesture and Lucie hastened towards her and took the proffered hands in hers. To her surprise, although they felt like physical objects, they had no warmth in terms of the normal skin to skin contact one would naturally expect. They didn't feel cold either, just inert somehow. Apart from registering this fact somewhere in her semi-conscious mind, Lucie was far too excited and immersed in the prospect of seeing her mother again to really take much notice of it or allow the registry of that information to proceed to the point of forming a question about the nature of who exactly she was dealing with. Instead, blinded by her own emotion and the anticipation of what lay ahead, she asked, panting slightly, "Where is my mum?"

"Follow me." Naamah turned effortlessly and seemed to glide off around the back of the keep. Lucie had not been round here before.

"I was told there was nothing around here," she stated. "Where are we going?"

Naamah did not need to reply, for there in the wall, not looking the least bit out of place or even hidden, was a door. Again, under normal circumstances, Lucie would probably have asked more questions, but there was nothing about the events which had just happened that made Lucie feel suspicious or nervous in any way. Naamah opened the door and beckoned Lucie in, and without hesitation, she followed.

The first thing that struck Lucie was that they were in a dark, tunnel-like corridor. It seemed very different from the other parts of the Castle that she had investigated. It was colder too, and she shivered involuntarily.

"Where does this go? Where are we exactly, I haven't been here before?" Lucie was starting to feel a little anxious, but she couldn't allow herself to doubt what Naamah had promised her.

"We are going to see your mother, like I said," Naamah responded, without slowing her pace.

At the end of the corridor there was a room. It was similar to those in the Castle in terms of its dimensions, except the stone was a hard, grey granite instead of the warm sandstone she was used to. There were no windows either. In the room there was a single chair, upon which sat Lucie's mother.

"Mum!" she ran over and hugged her mother. She looked just as Lucie remembered her. "I can't believe it's you!"

"Lucie, my Darling. You have grown up so!" her mother replied. Her voice sounded a little different and the way she talked was a bit odd, but Lucie put that down to her faded memory. She was so overwhelmed. She cried like her heart would break, releasing all the pent up pain of seven years of separation. The creature beneath the façade was another of Nixon's guides, his name was Shapeshifter. He secretly laughed to himself, relishing her pain, while externally, the figment of a woman hugged the clinging girl, stroking her hair and whispering sweet sentiments into her ear.

Chapter 33: Everything Comes with a Price

When her tears eventually subsided, Lucie looked up, smiling. "Thank you, Naamah, you have no idea what you have done for me. But why did you do it? Why did you give me my mum back?"

"I know how much you have missed your mother. You can come and visit her here any time. We want the Castle to be so much more than it is already. We want it to help people individually as well as collectively."

"Really? Any time?" Lucie was incredulous.

"Yes, my Love," her mother affirmed. "We can be together again."

"Wow! This is unreal! Wait till I tell Dad!"

"You can't tell him, I'm afraid Lucie," her mother responded, gravely. "You can't tell anyone. I can only be here for you, secretly."

"Oh, okay." She was a little disappointed that she couldn't share this joy with her father. She knew how tough it had been on him, too. She had heard him, when he thought she was asleep, she knew how much he had suffered through all this. He hadn't wanted to be a single parent, it had completely altered every aspect of his life. He needed love and hope too. But Lucie felt a selfish desire to do anything she could to be with her mother, and if she had to pay the price of keeping it from her dad, then she would.

And that is what Nixon was banking on. Now to find others with emotional leverage and he could proceed to the next phase of his plan. Lucie was his trump card though, and to save attracting any attention to himself, he would use her now to recruit others, knowing she would be willing to do virtually anything for one more hug from her mother; one more whispered 'I love you'.

On her second visit, which also took place during the night when the Castle was pretty much deserted, Naamah once again led her down the dark corridor. And, once again, her mother was waiting for her looking radiant and expectant. Lucie ran to her and they talked for ages about what Lucie was doing – at school, with friends, through clubs and interests. She exaggerated her happiness and sense of belonging, wanting her mum to be at ease about how well she had adjusted to her loss.

As Lucie got up to leave, her mother spoke to her in a more serious voice. "Lucie, Darling, can you do something for me?"

"Yes, what is it?" Lucie knelt down, looking up into her mother's face earnestly, desperate to do whatever she could within her power.

"Naamah has been so kind, leading you here to me. She needs some help in the Castle. They are trying to upgrade the rooms to allow for the new level of interaction we have been talking about. There are so many children like you who can be helped, if only the Castle gets the new doors installed. But they need assistance. Adults can be so driven and single minded about things, it takes children's thinking to really access the fullness of what is achievable. Do you think you could help, Darling? There are other children who need to be connected in just as you have been, but Naamah has so much to do that she needs helpers or they will fall behind. We need to make this our priority, then we can get together again after it is all sorted out. Will that be okay?"

"Of course, I will help in any way I can," she said. The sweet, imploring look on her mother's face was too much, how could Lucie refuse? "Especially after all you have done for me, Naamah," Lucie added, looking towards her guardian. At this point she hadn't really processed what was being asked of her; the fact that what her mother was actually saying was that they could not be together again until Lucie had brought in at least one other child to assist in whatever it was they were trying to achieve.

"Can you think of any one who you can bring along with you, Lucie?"

"Well, I don't really know anyone." Her face fell as she had to admit this to her mum. "I have other friends, of course, but I don't really know anyone in the Castle. I've not been coming for very long," she added, quickly, to save face.

"Don't worry," Naamah interjected – she already knew that Lucie was in no position to bring anyone, but giving her the option was a way of manipulating her in to thinking that she had been part of the whole decision making process on some level, to the point where she would be relieved to be assigned someone, if only to satisfy herself that she was able to meet her mother's request. It was a simple strategy, but it worked. "I will help to guide you in your choice," Naamah nobly suggested, smiling compassionately and bowing her head.

Lucie was relieved that the pressure to find a helper did not rest with her and readily agreed. She returned to her normal life and the following night she received a dream featuring Naamah again. On this occasion, there was little of the previous alluring atmosphere and beautiful surroundings; just Naamah's face and a name, followed by a reminder that seeing her mum again was dependant on her success.

Lucie woke up with a start, remembering the dream clearly, and the name: 'Jack Edwards'. She wrote it down, wondering to herself how she would ever be able to find him. Presumably he was already a member of the Collective? She would start tomorrow. The sooner she achieved this, the sooner she would be back with her mum. She tried to close her eyes and settle back to sleep, but she shivered in the cold gloom of the early hours and her eyes refused to shut. Naamah's face still seemed to hang in the shadows and it unsettled her. She tried to tell herself she was doing the right thing, this was for the greater good and had nothing to do with her own selfish desire to be with her mum. It would be of service to others like her, she told herself, it wasn't too much to ask; was it?

Chapter 34: Lucie's Plan

It was December again, and in spite of being in Year 11 and gearing up for his exams, Xander was spending an increasing amount of time at Scarlett's office. His parents were both busy with their separate ventures, so he had managed to retain the secrecy of his involvement in the Collective through a few well placed lies about revision groups and so on. Rosie had been hard at work too, following up on something she had felt was a valuable tool for the organisation – the compilation of a database of members of the Collective. Scarlett was particularly good at allowing them the freedom to pursue the things they felt passionate about. She was not controlling, or precious about the group and was more than willing to let others develop their ideas or aspire to things she may not have considered herself. It had involved a lot of work at the outset, as the Collective had grown to encompass about 200 members in all, and this number was constantly being added to with their rolling programme of engaging with news schools every week, meaning she was continually updating it. She was methodical and proficient with a computer, so Rosie had managed to gradually diminish the work involved through her efficiency.

Xander felt his strengths lay in structuring working parties, now that they had the numbers, assigned to national initiatives for each of the rooms. He wanted to see the reach of the Collective extended and people's vision within it increased so they were not just thinking on a micro level all of the time, but could raise their eyes to take in the macro possibilities. So far, they had a group which operated on a weekly basis out of the Family room (and this was headed up by Rosie, who had a real passion for seeing the role of family advancing once again within the community.) They would positively visualise strong and lasting partnerships, security and communication, a place where children could develop and reach their potential in a loving and supportive home. She believed that this was what every couple who embarked on having children ultimately wanted to achieve and felt it was important to stand with them in it. In Health – under the guidance of Dan – a team was concentrating on significantly reducing instances of life threatening conditions by visualising new research in to naturally occurring remedies, shorter waiting times and accurate diagnoses. The research charities and organisations developing cures for cancer, for example, were already determined to find solutions which would ultimately render the disease completely treatable and they backed them up with powerful waves of positive thought, engaging the Brightness to partner with them in something they felt it seemed to want to do anyway. Other global conditions were also targeted and Dan became quite an expert on various insidious diseases. Their latest project, to which Xander had assigned himself, was that of finances. He was spurred on by the success he had seen for his father, particularly, and had become more and more interested in economics as a subject. From what he picked up on news based websites, Xander was keen to see the radical move towards a fair distribution of funds, tax equality – especially where the multi-nationals were concerned – and realistic wages and welfare assistance. It was early days for this phase of the organisation, but they were all excited by the prospect of getting their teeth into something weighty, that may have real repercussions in the nation.

Xander stepped out of the Elevator to meet his new group in the Finances room – this was only the third week they had been operating like this and he was already delighted with the participants, all of which seemed to have a genuine desire to affect national policy and somehow find a way, guided by the Brightness, to steer the country away from its more recent financial pit falls and build something more stable and viable. He glanced up – as he had been doing more frequently over the last few weeks – at the sky. The cloud, which had remained innocuous, was now slightly larger, he judged, and was no longer pure white but had a negligible tinge of grey to the under side of it. Still nobody else had mentioned it, but having monitored it closely and noticed a change, Xander decided to disclose it to Scarlett at their next meeting.

In the courtyard, he noticed a plain looking girl he had seen around – always on her own. She was nervously shifting her weight from foot to foot.

"Hi. Xander isn't it?" she enquired, timidly, in a thin little voice that seemed too young for her.

"Yes. Hi, what's up?" He looked at his watch instinctively, not wanting to be late for his group.

"I met someone here last week. I don't have many friends and we hit it off. We worked on something together, but I haven't seen him for a few days and I wanted to tell him about the success we had had. Is there a way I can contact him?" Lucie looked hopefully at him. She didn't want to arouse any suspicion and felt this was the most plausible line of attack. Xander thought her speech seemed a little rehearsed, but he put it down to her being a bit anxious about talking to people. He felt sorry for her. She looked small and lonely, stood there in her school uniform, twisting her fingers together nervously. Her hair was tightly drawn back into a pony tail, which didn't really suit her features. Her imploring look made her eyes stand out in an unattractive bug-like fashion and he wondered to himself why her mother didn't help her more with her appearance; it made her a target for bullies, he thought. The fact that she had found someone to work with encouraged him. After all, if the Collective could not provide a safe environment for her to interact and build her confidence, what hope was there?

"My friend Rosie is compiling a database," he divulged at last. "Let me give you her number, I'm sure she'll be able to help you." Xander took out his phone adeptly and read Rosie's number to Lucie, who typed it in to her own mobile. He walked off, smiling to himself at the thought of bringing a couple of introverts together. Lucie smiled too, but hers was more triumphant than benevolent, "I'm nearly there Mum, wait for me," she said quietly to herself, knowing she was one step closer than she had been moments ago.

Chapter 35: Jack

"Well done, Lucie, that was very resourceful of you," said Naamah in a congratulatory tone. Lucie jumped and spun around, she hadn't seen her approach.

"What do I do when I've found Jack?"

"Just bring him to the Family room, like you were told," said Naamah. Lucie thought she detected the smallest note of irritation in her voice and it surprised her. Naamah was usually so gentle. She decided it must be because of how busy she was with the restructuring, it was a massive responsibility. It made her want to help. She turned her back on Naamah to call Rosie.

After a couple of rings, Rosie answered in an efficient tone. "Hi, Rosie's phone. Who's this?"

"Xander gave me your number," Lucie explained, going straight in with the information she though was most likely to secure a speedy result. "My name is Lucie and I'm a member of the Collective. I'm trying to trace Jack Edwards. Xander thought you could help me, he mentioned the database." She held her breath, expectantly.

"Did he. Right. I can help, yes. But why do you need his number? I'm not sure I should be passing out member's details without a good reason." Rosie sounded quite serious and Lucie admired her for her commitment.

She fell back on the lie she had used with Xander. "We were working on something together the other day and he really helped me. I wanted to let him know about the positive outcome. I don't really know anyone in the Collective, if I'm honest, and it would be really good to work with somebody regularly."

Like Xander, Rosie agreed that this was one of the aims for the Collective; to get people who previously would not know each other working together for a common cause. She saw no harm in it. "Sure, okay. I don't have the number on me at the moment, but I can stop by the office tomorrow and look it up. I'll text it to you."

Lucie's rational mind knew this was more than she could have hoped for, to get such a positive result so quickly – it was really kind of Rosie to be so accommodating, she reminded herself. But emotionally, she wanted things sorted right now so she was free to see her mum. Why were they making her wait? She wondered, petulantly. "Yeah, thanks, that's great," she managed to say and hung up.

Rosie stared at her phone and raised her eyebrows, puzzled. "Bye then," she said and put it back in to her blazer pocket.

It was not until four o'clock the next afternoon that the long awaited text finally appeared on Lucie's phone, with a mobile number for Jack Edwards. With trembling hands, Lucie selected the number and rang it. Four rings, "Come on, come on. Pick up!" she urged.

"Hello?" A boy's voice; young and uncertain.

"Is that Jack?" Lucie's question did nothing to dispel his suspicion.

"Yeah. Who's this?"

"My name's Lucie. I was asked to meet you in the Family Room by someone high up in the Collective. They gave me your number and asked me to call. I think it's quite urgent, they want to get a group together. Are you free now?"

"What's it all about?" he asked, still sounding sceptical.

"I really don't know any more than you," Lucie said truthfully. "Can you help?"

"I suppose. Can we do it at six though, I've just got in?"

"Should be okay. I'll meet you there at six. Thanks."

"Bye." He hung up.

Lucie's heart was beating fast; she was so far out of her comfort zone. What was she getting herself into? Naamah was her guardian, she was there to look after her. And her mum wouldn't allow anything to happen to her, she reassured herself. She was overreacting, everything was going to be fine. Wasn't it?

Chapter 36: Six O'clock

At a quarter to six that evening, Lucie arrived in the Family Room to wait for Jack. Mercifully, there was nobody else in the room, so she closed the door and paced around, nervously. She found herself walking around the labyrinth pattern on the floor as if she was a young child again, balancing on a low wall and concentrating, foot in front of foot, to maintain that balance and not fall off. When she tired of that, she walked around the perimeter of the room, trailing her hand along the smooth stones that made up the sandstone wall. She was suddenly aware of a crevice in the rock. She examined it more closely and realised it was quite a large, vertical crack that almost reached the ceiling before turning at right angles and meandering along on the horizontal plane for a while. It then turned downwards, perpendicular to the second line and made its way directly to the floor. It was a doorway, almost invisible to the naked eye it was so well camouflaged and she realised that she would not have spotted it at all if she had not been touching the stone. She put her fingers to the crack again and felt the tiniest blast of air being emitted from the gap, before being aware of a muffled sound behind it. Suddenly, the door opened out in to the room, and would have hit her if she hadn't jumped back quickly. Naamah walked in with another person she had not seen before and they seemed a little surprised to see her there already. They appeared to share a brief, secretive glance with each other and Lucie felt like an intruder. He was a young man, with the same kind of innate beauty and light about him as Naamah. He must be Jack's guardian, she reasoned to herself.

"Hello," she said, more boldly than she felt. "Who are you?"

"I'm Hanun, gracious and merciful; at your service." He bowed in a low, exaggerated fashion which made Lucie smile.

"And I'm Lucie, confused and ignorant," she quipped. They both stared at her, blankly. They might be gorgeous people, but they sure lacked a sense of humour, she thought to herself. "Can either of you tell me what's going on?" She looked at them, hopefully. But her joke had not broken the ice and their expressions did not change. Lucie was just beginning to feel a little awkward when the main door opened and Jack walked in.

"Hi, are you Lucie?" he enquired.

"Yes, thanks for coming," she said, relieved – and expectant that now she would finally get some answers and be able to move on from all of this to see her mum.

"So, why are we here? Who are they?" He pointed to the guardians. Lucie was about to speak, but Naamah put her finger to her lips and Hanun spoke instead.

"I am your guardian, Jack. We are a recent addition to the Castle. Now that things have stepped up, we have been allowed to come in to protect you all. Some of us have just one child in our charge, but others have several assigned to them. Naamah and I are here to look after the special ones. Not everyone has the ability to make a high level of impact in this realm, but you two are unique, you have a gift. Because of this, you need special protection or you could become a target for all kinds of dangers which lie ahead. Do not be alarmed, we are here to help you, to watch over you. We have seen something in your future, Jack, and I have come to warn you. Your father works for the Foreign Office, does he not?"

"Yes, why? What's up?" Jack looked alarmed and his voice rose as he spoke.

"Are you aware that your father has been posted out to the Middle East?"

"There was talk of it, but I don't think it's been confirmed yet."

"It has. He knows and I'm sure he will talk to you about it soon. What troubles us is that we have seen a tragedy in his future which could send out ripples across the world, not just the nation. In these early days of establishing the Collective, we want to ensure that there is every possible opportunity for it to succeed. It will transform this land, but only with our intervention. Do you believe in the Collective, Jack?"

"Yes, I do. But what's this about my dad? I don't really understand what you're saying."

"I'm saying that there is a terrorist attack on the Embassy where your father is to be posted, being planned at this moment. They are high level, well funded and organised operatives. They are also well hidden within the establishment and we need your help to expose them. Normally we would try to influence things without involving you, but it is imminent and potentially devastating. We need to engage you and draw on your collective minds to foil this plan. It is not just your father's life we want to protect, Jack. Can you see the urgency?"

"Yes I can, but why can't we just tell the government? Surely they have the power to stop this. Let me warn my dad, he'll know what to do."

"They won't take you seriously, Jack. How are you going to explain what you know? This is the only way."

"I can visualise him safe, can't I?" He seemed desperate.

"We shouldn't really be talking to you about this. The Collective was designed to alter what is already in place and visualise a new hope, it was not meant to respond to predictions about the future. We are not meant to change the course of what will one day be history, if you can see the subtle difference. But when we saw this, we couldn't bear to see you and so many others suffer such loss. Lucie understands, that's why we called on her to help, she lost her mother."

Jack looked at Lucie. His face was etched with the horror of the moment, but she caught the familiar sight of sympathy. "I'm sorry," he said. She shrugged and smiled at him. After a few seconds, Jack turned his gaze back to the guardians. "What do I need to do?"

"Come with us, Jack. You are doing the right thing."

"What about me?" Lucie asked. "What should I do? Can I go and see Mum now?"

Naamah shot her a brief glance of irritation and Lucie realised she had mentioned her mum, the big secret. "In a while. Please come with us," Naamah said, silkily, recovering her composure, but not her compassion. "We still need your help."

The new door opened again and the four of them entered into a dark corridor.

"Where does this go?" Jack asked.

"The future."

Chapter 37: Counter-terrorism

“Welcome.” It was Peter Nixon. Lucie did a double take, surprised to see him sitting there in such a fashion, on a large chair which she thought was almost throne-like. It was an extensive room in the same grey granite as the one where she had met her mum, but more palatial in its dimensions and design – although not exactly comfortable or welcoming. There was nowhere for them to sit, so they stood before him, seated as he was on a slightly raised platform.

“We are extending the Castle,” he said, making a sweeping gesture with his hand. “This area is for specially selected people to come and engage with important issues. Scarlett has done a wonderful job, but her ambitions are limited and her vision falls short as she does possess a certain airy-fairy, romantic quality, shall we say." He wafted his hand dismissively. "We are alarmed by the stance the current government is taking against terrorism and we feel we have a moral duty to the nation to step up our influence here to protect people. They are cutting the defence budget and laying off the armed forces; security policy has been relaxed in the wake of a period of relative calm and trading agreements are a complete farce – I tell you all of this in confidence you understand?” He seemed passionate, maybe even a little over zealous, Lucie thought, as she looked at him sat on his ‘throne’ waving his arms about in wild gesticulations. He went on, “The Collective has done a lot to stabilise this nation and bring about a new found peace and hope for the future, but it has also allowed people to become sloppy and careless. Things have been permitted to develop unseen while the nation parties and lives it up, but the time has come for us to stand against this new enemy in collective visualisation. We cannot afford to let our guard down, otherwise, who knows what might happen?" There was a slightly wild glint in his eye at this point, as he left the sentence hanging.

"I thought this was about my father?" Jack interjected. "About foiling the terror plot?"

"And so it is my boy, so it is. What Hanun saw for your father is a symptom of the policy I was just talking about. We need to nip this in the bud."

"But how, exactly, can we stop them? I know visualisation works best when we are specific. What do we really know?" Jack felt a pang of fear. He was worried that they had promised him something they couldn't deliver – the safety of his father.

"We have seen the terror attack, Jack. But we don't know who the perpetrators are. They are well hidden as I said before. We can go some way to visualising their exposure, but our most effective course of action would undoubtedly be to seek the replacement of the policy makers – not the government itself, obviously, just those making key decisions over national security. We need a new leadership; people with the right motives and the best interests of this nation at heart." Hanun spoke with conviction.

This made sense to Lucie, she was keen to support Jack so he didn't have to go through what she had – the loss of a parent. Jack himself still looked shocked, he was struggling to take it all in. "What should we do?" she asked, looking at Jack with solidarity and reassurance.

"Jack, you have authority here as it affects you personally. Hanun can work for you, what would you like him to do?"

"Take out the policy makers," Jack said, decisively, his mouth set in a grim line of determination. "We can't let them waste this country. Replace them with people who can be trusted to ensure our national security."

Nixon had a satisfied expression on his face as he beckoned them to come close and join hands in a circle. "Let us visualise it together," he said, solemnly.

The five of them, as one, called for the very thing which Jack had just said. The children, naively, did not register the potential horror of Jack's words – which Nixon was keen for them to use exactly as he and spoken them – but they felt the awesome power generated between them and, at its pinnacle, Hanun left the room. Neither of the children noticed that, for the first time operating in this realm, an agreement had been made with one distinct absence; the Brightness had not featured in their petition.

"It is done," Peter Nixon looked contented. He knew the line had been crossed and he was now free to implement his own agenda. "Thank you. Your father will be safe."

Lucie and Jack found themselves back in the Family Room, a little dazed and not quite sure what had just happened. They went their separate ways without speaking, there was nothing to say. Little did they know the extent of what had just been accomplished and the gateway it had allowed to what was to come. A new order had been established and they had naively ushered it in.

As Jack walked back towards the Elevator, Lucie ducked around the back of the keep to find the doorway that would take her to her mother. It was gone.

Chapter 38: A National Disaster

Xander made the decision that he could wait no longer to talk to Scarlett about the clouds and he went straight to her office after school. He couldn't shake the feelings he had concerning these clouds, he was apprehensive but he didn't know if he was imagining things or just making something out of nothing. At the end of the day, this was new for everyone, even Scarlett, so nobody could really predict how things would pan out or what would develop along the way. It was such an awkward juxtaposition, for on the one hand there was a real buzz about the office; people were working on press releases as remarkable things were taking place across the nation on a daily basis; proposals were being drafted up and continually developed and refined and new connections were being made and pathways forged in to alternative and exciting areas all the time. What Scarlett had achieved here was truly astonishing. Yet, something was wrong, Xander sensed it, and it was not a tangible thing. It bore no relation to all of the outward signs of success, it was a gut feeling; a 'disturbance in the force' if you like. Would she listen to him though, a fifteen year old boy? He had a good relationship with her and he trusted her, but would she be willing to hear what he had to say? All of these thoughts and questions had been whirling around his head for days, not just on the tube over here, or the elevator ride up to her office. This was not a fanciful notion that he was acting upon in haste.

"Hi Xander. You look like you're miles away!" It was Jess, Scarlett's receptionist, looking at him with a quizzical expression on her face. "You're not in the book, hon. She's in a meeting at the moment, can it wait?"

"No, it can't," Xander replied, firmly. He had made his decision, in that split second he knew he could not let it go. "But I can," he added, and made his way over to one of the easy chairs outside her office to sit it out.

He could hear the low murmur of voices coming from inside the room, with the occasional word more heavily articulated. Sometimes the dialogue – for he had decided he could only identify two different voices – was punctuated with a laugh or a slight cough. He was almost certain that the other voice belonged to a man, but it was more muffled than Scarlett's more recognisable voice. He glanced at his watch. He had only been waiting for about ten minutes, but it felt more like thirty and he shifted his weight on the decorative - but hardly designed to be sat upon – chair he had selected. Finally, the door opened and Peter Nixon came out. He looked at Xander and there was a flash of recognition in his eyes. Xander had meant to stand up, but was momentarily paralysed, feeling himself blush – almost as though he was guilty of something, which was ridiculous – under the gaze of this man. What was it about Nixon that caused so many different reactions within him? The politician paused in his stride for a second or two, nodded curtly at Xander, then moved off purposefully towards the elevators.

"Xander, hi, sorry to keep you. Go on in, I'll be back in a moment." He had almost forgotten why he was there, or even who he was there to see, flustered as he was by seeing Nixon again. In the early days, he had seen him around the Castle from time to time, always busy and efficient, moving between certain rooms. But it occurred to him then that it had been several months since he had seen him on anything other than the television or newspapers. He stood up, trying to shake off the uneasy sensations which had only been added to in the past few moments, and walked in to Scarlett's office.

It was a bright, colourful room with large areas of glazing – not with any particular view, but it was good to look out across the city from this elevated position. Xander sat down on a red sofa located under one of the windows and in front of a large flat screen television mounted on the wall at the other end of the room from Scarlett's desk. The television was on, but muted, and was set – as it always seemed to be – to one of the twenty-four hour news channels. Suddenly the picture shifted from a stricken looking studio anchor to a location reporter looking flustered in front of the House of Commons. As the winter solstice was fast approaching, daylight was draining away from the sky behind her, but it was still possible to see – all too clearly – that smoke was billowing out of the building. The twilight also accentuated the eerie blue flashing lights of emergency vehicles, some of which were still approaching the scene. It was chaos. The banner along the bottom of the screen read:

Breaking News: Suspected terrorist attack at House of Commons. Unspecified casualties.

Xander reached for the remote and pressed the mute button just as Scarlett re-entered the room. He couldn't speak. He was transfixed by what was on the screen before him and the clamour of disaster emanating from it.

"A little after three o'clock this afternoon, there was an explosion in the House of Commons. Reports are sketchy at this time, but Parliament was in session." The reporter was desperately trying to maintain her professionalism in what was undoubtedly the biggest story of her career. She was not one of their flagship reporters, it could only be assumed that she happened to be on location reporting on something much more mundane when all hell literally broke lose. She kept pressing the device in her ear, desperate to hear above the wail of sirens, any form of instruction from her producer. "We are unclear at this time how many are injured, but we have had reports to indicated that there are casualties at the scene. At this time, the cause of the explosion is unclear. No group or faction has yet come forward to claim responsibility for it – it is still possible that it may just be a tragic accident." Although the expression on her face contradicted the words that came out of her mouth. "We will bring you more on this as it comes in. Back to James in the studio."

Scarlett stood with her hand to her mouth in horror at the unfolding scene. "Oh my God," she muttered. "How could this happen?" Mechanically, she sank in to a chair near Xander. They continued to watch in silence for a few minutes.

The anchor, having basically repeated what the reporter had just said, also fiddled with his earpiece before asking the question, "Cathy, there are unconfirmed reports reaching us that the Prime Minister may be injured. What can you tell us about that?"

The location reporter seemed to have gained some of her composure after the initial shock of having to break such a big story. "Yes, James, we have heard that the Prime Minister was one of those injured in the blast, along with the Chancellor and the Home Secretary. It seems that what ever it was that triggered this horrific event, its epicentre was close to where the PM sits in the House with his closest advisors. This knowledge makes the likelihood of some kind of terrorist or malicious motive all the more plausible, I'm afraid."

Scarlett suddenly stood up and turned to Xander. "I'm sorry Xander, you'll have to go. Whatever it was you wanted to talk about will have to wait I'm afraid. I must convene with the Inner Circle over this. We must see what we can do to limit the damage here. I can't believe this is happening. How could it?" She had turned and was already walking towards the door. "I'll see you soon," and she was gone.

He had no choice but to go too. But that didn't mean this had to wait. He decided, on his way down in the lift, to call Rosie and Dan and head for the Castle as well. Something told him this was not the work of terrorists, but that something much more sinister was going on. But who would do such a monstrous thing?

Chapter 39: Suspicions

"Meet me in the Elevator in five minutes. It's important, I want to show you something." Xander spoke urgently into his phone as he slammed the front door of his house against the chill winter gloom, dropped his bag in the hall and ascended the staircase without stopping to check if anyone was home. He needed to be somewhere safe, where he could close the door on this world and enter into the other through visualisation.

"Hi, nice to speak to you too. I'm fine, thanks for asking! What's up? You sound weird," Rosie responded.

"Tell you when I see you, no time," he said, abruptly into his handset and hung up before having an almost identical – but not quite as heavy on the sarcasm – conversation with Dan. Guys were so much easier, he thought. No small talk, straight to the point. He allowed himself a brief smile, he had to admit he did like that side of Rosie's character, frustrating as it was at times.

"So what's going on, man?" Dan asked, as the three of them rode up together in the Elevator.

"You'll see," said Xander, enigmatically, his jaw set and his eyes firmly forward, concentrating on the doors. They opened and he stepped out first. He turned round to face them as they followed him out. "What do you see?" he challenged them.

"What do you mean? What I always see when I come up here. What's got in to you?"

Xander started speaking over Rosie before she had finished what she was saying, raising his voice rudely above hers. "LOOK!" he commanded. "What do you SEE?"

Rosie shrank back a little from the harshness of his words and he hated how he had made her feel, but it did have the desired effect. She turned away from Xander and looked around her with the eye of a connoisseur. "I don't see anything unusual . . . . wait. What? Do you mean those clouds?"

There were two distinct forms now, undoubtedly darker than before and bigger. Quite a bit bigger, he thought, upon reflection. "Yes! Those clouds!" he answered, relieved that she could see them.

"What about them, mate?" Dan asked, nonchalantly. "What's the biggie?"

"Can't you feel it?" Xander asked, knowing he sounded a bit desperate. Was he going mad? "Something's wrong. Something's changed."

"I don't know, they're just clouds. Don't you think you might be over reacting just a tad?" Dan looked at him with a measure of concern in his eyes.

Unperturbed, Xander ploughed on. He had to make them see. "There weren't any until a couple of weeks ago when a small white one appeared. Think about it, we've been coming here for a year and this was the first cloud in all that time. It has to signal something has changed. Its colour altered fairly soon after that and now there are two. I don't pretend to know what it means, only that it means something I just know it, and I don't like it. Trust me on this, I've given it a lot of thought and I keep coming back to the same place, and it's not pretty, believe me!"

"They're clouds, mate! It could just mean that it's going to rain!" Dan quipped.

Xander looked at Rosie for reassurance, with an exasperated expression on his face. She felt it too, he could see it in her eyes. He relaxed a little.

"You're right. There were no clouds for a whole year, so why now? It could be positive, like rain brings nourishment and refreshing?" She was trying to put a pragmatic spin on things, and Xander appreciated her efforts, but they both knew that this wasn't about rain.

"I don't think it's about rain," he voiced it and could see she agreed. Dan still appeared to be somewhat out of the loop, but he had picked up on their commonly held belief and tried to graft his thinking in to theirs.

"Maybe there's a storm coming?" Dan suggested, casually. They were simple words, but they struck Xander with force.

"I think you might be on to something there," he agreed, grimly.

Rosie felt it too and nodded her assent. "Has Scarlett seen them?" she asked, looking anxiously at the boys.

"I don't know. I went to talk to her just now, then the news came on. They're up in the Throne Room this moment, trying to minimise the damage. I can't be certain, but I think it's all connected somehow."

"You think what's connected? What news?" Rosie asked, puzzled. Dan looked equally mystified.

"Didn't you hear? Someone tried to blow up the House of Commons!"

Chapter 40: Inner Circle

Scarlett was never ambivalent about the assembly of power within the Throne Room. Three cabinet ministers now held seats – thanks to a couple of recent introductions by Peter – along with a board member at the Bank of England and a leading NHS boss. Scarlett had wanted to have people in situ who reflected the main focus of the rooms within the Castle and they had gone a long way over the last six months particularly, to make that wish a reality.

"By now I am sure you are all aware of the tragic events at Westminster," she said, by way of introduction, speaking over the last of the buzz that had permeated the room while everyone had been arriving. Even people in high positions can't help discussing tragic events, there is an inbuilt voyeur in most of us.

"I would have been there too, if I hadn't had that meeting with you," Peter interjected, looking shaken. He looked pointedly at Scarlett, who nodded back, sympathetically.

"Are there any more details?" asked one of the members.

"The PM has not yet regained consciousness, but he was mercifully still alive. The latest report was that five people were pronounced dead at the scene – including the Speaker. At least ten more have been hospitalised with various degrees of injury." It was John Davis, one of the other cabinet members. He currently sat on the Agriculture Committee and had escaped the drama of the House due to a scheduling clash with a meeting elsewhere in the building. A murmur of shock rippled around the room like a Mexican wave, closely followed by a pungent silence.

"What can we do?" asked Michael Lawrence, CEO of a large pharmaceutical company. It was the question upon everyone's lips. They all felt equally helpless and shaken by the events which were so close to home and contrasted so sharply with the wave of optimistic excitement they had been riding for months.

"We need to get on top of this before it derails the future for this organisation and the nation. Priority number one is to focus on the wellbeing of all of those caught up in the blast," Scarlett declared, taking on a masterful tone and leading the group who all felt agitated and distressed by the events they had witnessed. "Secondly, we need to preserve the leadership of this country. So many positive things have taken place recently, we mustn't allow ourselves to be distracted from our goal. We were heading somewhere really positive and have seen a new level of national unity. We don't want to lose that now."

The Inner Circle of the Collective joined together with renewed vigour, unaware that there was already division within their ranks. All but one, spurred on by a sense of national pride and the mutual horror of what had occurred, focused like never before on getting the country back on its feet and minimising the legacy it would undoubtedly leave in its wake. Nixon played along, all the while hiding the delight he felt at being one step closer to the power he craved. It had been a stroke of genius to use the children, but he had needed to put in a huge amount of preparation to get to this point. He mused to himself about Scarlett's reasons for engaging young people in the first place – to inspire them, to give them hope and a vision for their future. But what she had overlooked, what he now understood, was that children seemed to possess a greater level of purity which made their thoughts so much more potent. Their faith in the visualisations they engendered was unpolluted by the lack of belief adults seem to carry around on their shoulders like a pirate's parrot; whispering to them and discouraging them. This faith had served him well; it had served Moloch well – as the way Nixon had re-engineered the Castle meant that Moloch was sated by the powerful exchanges which took place. The Brightness had been side-stepped, eliminated from the equation. As such, the balance of power had shifted and with it the regulation of a benevolent force. Now darkness had its foot in the door, it would brood and grow, like the storm that Dan had unwittingly predicted. It was win,

win, as far as Nixon was concerned. Nothing or nobody was going to stop him now.

"Le roi est mort, vive le roi!" he said to himself – suddenly finding himself quoting a saying he had learned in A Level History – "The King is dead, long live the king!" He was glad, more than ever before, that they sat facing away from each other. For whilst the others focussed with a dedicated fervour on doing good, Nixon sat, leaning back in his chair, with a satisfied smile playing across his lips.

Chapter 41: Developments

Over the next few days, the chaos that had struck right at the heart of government gradually began to subside and some sort of order was established. The security services and the police had been working day and night to try to determine exactly what had happened on that fateful day. In the first instance there was a good deal of confusion, as their prime suspect was a workman who had been contracted with a small group of others to do some routine maintenance work. The issue lay with the fact that he maintained he had not been at work that day, yet he had been clearly identified on the state of the art security system. The group had worked at the Parliament buildings before – indeed they were routinely used and had been rigorously checked. Strangely though, this one particular man had called in sick that morning – and there was a recording of the call he made. Although at the time nobody became suspicious of the fact that he appeared to turn up for work anyway, it was later the main reason for focusing on him as a suspect. His colleagues thought he had been hung-over after a rather raucous night out to celebrate a birthday on the previous evening, but that he had decided to stick it out after all – he was not himself, they testified, much quieter than usual. But after the event, when he was interviewed by the authorities, he was adamant that he had not gone in at all that day. This led to a short spell in custody with some attempts to 'encourage' him to tell the truth, but he stuck to his story. He had actually attended his local surgery with fears of a particularly violent bout of food poisoning, and this proved to be his saving grace as they could not only verify that someone answering to his name had been present at an appointment on that day, it appeared that they had a covert surveillance system in operation to ensure the safety of their practitioners! The event caused quite a stink in the press – a violation of people's rights where the surgery was concerned, but also the security breach at the highest level that allowed someone to impersonate a worker and enter the government headquarters unchallenged. Ultimately the police had no choice but to let the workman go, without prosecution – there was no apology either, but he was just relieved to be out of the nightmare, so did not push for one. The man on the CCTV footage bore an uncanny resemblance to him, so much so that without the evidence from the surgery and testimony of his family, the poor man would probably still be under lock and key in a dark basement somewhere, undergoing interview techniques adapted and perfected during the war on terror. This impostor had not been seen or heard from since. He was last observed taking a comfort break shortly before the explosion, by one of the other members of their workforce. And so the trail had – to the intense embarrassment of all concerned – gone cold.

The Prime Minister remained in a coma with extensive burns – it did not look good for him, but nevertheless the country continued its vigil for his recovery. There had been an emergency reshaping of the cabinet, which saw Peter Nixon temporarily assume the position of acting Prime Minister – as the Deputy Prime Minister was one of the casualties still on the critical list. His associates, John Davis and Michael Whitshaw, were also moved to new positions as Chancellor of the Exchequer and Home Secretary after the sad demise of the previous post holders. Nixon thrived on the celebrity of his new position, giving heartfelt interviews to the national press and encouraging the country to get behind him and the new cabinet as they did everything in their power to restore order and faith. He was the epitome of tact and compassion, striking the prefect balance between reassuring the country that he would bring the perpetrators to justice and gushing with sympathy for those who had been killed or injured and their families. When something of this magnitude takes place, it rocks the nation and causes fear. It was the fear that Nixon wanted to maintain, for it was the fear which would feed his plan and allow him to influence things that would previously have been off limits. People under attack withdraw and defend and he was certain that all of the recent positive drive and unity which the Collective had brought about, could be undermined with very little effort on his part. A few choice words, a home truth here or a leaked document there and the country would be willing to do whatever he suggested to protect themselves.

Behind the scenes, Nixon was progressing ever closer to his plan. Shapeshifter had served him well, assuming the identity of the maintenance man to throw up confusion and ultimately lead the authorities to a dead end. He smiled to himself, a useful addition to his team. No doubt he would find many more uses for him in the time to come. He had no qualms about what he was doing, in his own mind it made perfect sense. A megalomaniac does not stop to wonder whether he is hurting anyone's feelings along the way. It did not trouble him that he had used two innocent children to escalate his plan. Having used them, he abandoned them to the knowledge of what they had played a part in.

Lucie knew she had been manipulated and she was angry with herself for being so gullible; for being such a victim. She still did not understand how they had managed to involve her mum in the plan – she had no idea it was a shape shifter who had assumed the role. It never occurred to her that it had been anything other than her mum, so desperate was she to believe she had been allowed that small amount of extra time. She assumed they had used and manipulated her mother - or her spirit somehow – just as they had done with Lucie herself. It was probably for the best, as the poor girl would have struggled to cope with the truth and all that meant in terms of the sinister defilement of a child's most precious relationship – that of her parent. It reopened the old wound of loss and abandonment, bringing a desolation to her soul which she had previously learnt to contain. She felt that she needed to make some kind of response to what had happened, once she had gone through the range of emotions from shock and bewilderment; to anger and frustration; to hurt and mortification and finally to sadness and resolve. She tried to contact Jack to discuss with him what they should do about it. It wasn't that simple, unfortunately. Jack was in denial. He had changed his mobile number and dropped out of the Collective. He had managed to convince himself that he had saved his father's life; that he had no choice – how else could a young boy reconcile himself to the horror of what he had been a party to?

It was about a week after his first attempt, that Xander finally managed to get time with Scarlett – what with his school schedule in the run up to Christmas and her commitment to supporting Peter in what she thought was a play for national stability.

"Xander, good to see you again, come on in." She stood, holding the door open with her left hand, power-dressed in some killer heels and a red suit dress. She was smiling but, unusually for Scarlett, it didn't reach her eyes. The wan-ness of her complexion and the shadows around her features told a very different story – it had been such a shock to her after all of the positive signs, that in all honesty she was still reeling.

He walked in, feeling almost guilty that he was about to add to her troubles. "Thanks for seeing me Scarlett, I know you've been busy."

"I always try to make time for my protégées," she replied, with a little laugh. "What's on your mind?"

"Can't you tell?" he quipped, laughing at the rather old, in-house joke.

She had guided him towards her desk, obviously in the middle of something and keen to get straight back to it after he had left. As she spoke, she lowered herself down in to the leather swivel chair that Xander had secretly always wanted to sit at. He had sat down already in the chair opposite and looked intently at her while she settled herself. She hadn't even appeared to notice his poor attempt at humour and he wanted to make sure he had her attention before proceeding.

"Have you seen the clouds at the Castle?"

"I have, yes." This answer surprised him a little. But what had he expected? Someone like Scarlett, who took the care she did over all things relating to the Collective was hardly going to miss a new development, was she? So then why hadn't she mentioned it? Maybe she had; just not to him. There it was! That was what bothered him about her reply. He felt a twinge of jealousy that she hadn't mentioned it to him. But why would she? He was a kid!

He recovered himself and tried to remain focused. "What's caused them?"

"I don't know, Xander. But I'm sure it's nothing to worry about." She didn't look overly concerned, he thought.

"I think it is. I've watched them change. There were three yesterday and they are definitely getting bigger; and darker."

"This is all new for all of us, Xander. But I can assure you, there is nothing to worry about. I have an excellent team around me and I was very careful when I designed the Castle to ensure that it could not be corrupted by people misusing it."

"But how can you be sure?" Xander urged. "There are over two hundred members now. How can you be sure that at least one of them is not working with some harmful agenda?"

"Your imagination has run a little wild on this one. The Collective is a beautiful thing; a benevolent thing. It is designed to bless and transform; to build up people and communities. I keep a close eye on all that goes on in it. Now, don't you worry so much, that's my job!" She smiled reassuringly at him and it went some way to alleviating the anxiety he felt – although it did not dispel it completely. "How's your working party coming along?" It was a strategic and very deliberate change of subject on Scarlett's behalf and Xander had no choice but to respect the fact that that part of the conversation was over. He took her cue and talked, briefly, about his involvement in the group on finances. Everything seemed to be in a state of flux since the terror attack and they were all adjusting to new agendas in their various groups.

He left the room about five minutes later feeling he had done his best to warn her, but after all, he was a kid; she was the grown up. He had to trust her. He did trust her, he decided, as he walked towards the elevators to go back down to ground level, and home. But that didn't mean that he had to ignore what he increasingly felt was a dangerous and ominous symbol of what was to come.

Chapter 42: Christmas

It was amazing how quickly the new government clamped down on people's liberty. Fear was a wonderful partner to their new regime. Following the events at the Houses of Parliament, the new Home Secretary had introduced an identity card for all members of society, which carried a frightening amount of personal information – it would still take a little time to issue them, as it would be everyone from secondary school age and upwards, and issuing almost sixty million cards was no easy task. The fact that it had been passed at all would have been unthinkable even a few weeks before. Curfews were in place on the streets after eleven o'clock in the evening, making the capital – particularly – like some Middle Eastern country under martial law. People could be arrested on sight if they were out between that time and six in the morning without a valid reason. The Chancellor was putting measures in place to restrict financial transactions. This was being achieved through mobile phone technology, to eradicate the need for cash. The argument in favour of this was that people would be accountable at all times for what they did and more easily monitored by law. It had its critics too, who bemoaned the loss of personal freedom and a big brother attitude towards government. But the people were scared and Nixon had very subtly and with devastating results, fed that fear in order to implement his changes more quickly. The Fear was like a mythical dragon. In times of peace people were ambivalent about such things and assigned them to the realm of fantasy. However, we all have an invisible bond with this monster unless we choose to sever it and Nixon knew how to carefully tug on those chords leading back to the dragon of Fear and he pulled it decisively into the realm of reality. He understood how to play on people's superstitious and irrational tendencies when the ground they are standing on suddenly and unmistakeably shifts and crumbles and being the master of manipulation that he was, he sought to have his plans in place by Easter.

The happy Christmas he had had the year before seemed a long way off to Xander. Dad's business, which had been doing so well, had been hit by the curfew restrictions – afraid to be caught out of doors, or even afraid to be out in public places full stop, fewer people were spending evenings out. The limits on finances just added more to this burden – taxes had been increased to fund the changes and businesses were required to have very strict employment agreements and surveillance systems. Almost overnight, he had gone from running a successful business to being on his knees financially, and he looked more stressed than Xander had seen him for a long time. It was devastating for Xander, who couldn't help feeling a twinge of guilt about it as he had, after all, driven him forwards through visualisation. As well as what he saw happening at home and around the city, Xander was also alarmed by the deterioration he was witnessing within the Castle. The clouds had continued to build with frightening rapidity, to a point where they couldn't fail to be noticed anymore. With that was the ominous sense of foreboding. The cloud cover seemed to be affecting the success of visualisations. At times, it was nigh on impossible to even call up a picture from the Brightness, as a shadow was falling across the Castle – let alone actually see results for the things they were hoping to influence. There was an increasing sense of unease and paranoia around the Castle as more people noticed the difficulties with communications. Xander felt no sense of pride or sanctimonious pleasure from the fact that he had been right all along.

It was dimly lit in the basement of the Temple, where Nixon knelt before the beast he worshipped. "The plan is progressing well, Master," he informed Moloch, bowing low at his feet.

Moloch sat on his throne with his arms outstretched as usual, there was a faint sulphurous smell emitting from him. He looked down at his most loyal and fruitful subject with his ruby-red eyes. "What is your next step?" he asked, his voice coarse and grating.

"To take control of the Collective. We have the people under our sovereignty now, ruling through fear as you suggested, Master."

Moloch allowed himself a little smile of satisfaction. "Yes," he said. "Fear is a beautiful servant. How do you propose to take control?"

"Scarlett has been naive, she has left it too late to redeem her vision. My guides have infiltrated all of the rooms now, using children like Lucie and Jack, children with a weakness for people. Oh how I love the way they love – so pure, so trusting, so complete."

"I want that love, Peter. I want them for myself," Moloch petitioned him, a fleck of saliva becoming airborne as he spoke.

"And you will get it, Master. When they realise they can no longer operate in the Collective – and many of them are already becoming frustrated by the interference in the energy there – they will look for a way to continue to influence things. Scarlett gave us a wonderful gift by awakening their desire for change. All we need to do now is guide them this way. Naamah is good at that, she does deception so well!" He smiled as he said this, proud of his operatives and the seriousness with which they took their tasks. "Shapeshifter too will be invaluable to us. I have a plan in mind for him, I have asked him to take on a very special role, but not yet, we must bide our time Master. It is coming to us, we must not rush and try to make it happen."

"I like it!" Moloch declared. "You have thought of everything. It is so refreshing to work with someone of your calibre; someone who appreciates the subtleties of the way I operate. I have seen many come and go over the years. Some have left their mark, but most fall disappointingly short. Even the ones you think will go all the way - young Adolph for example, or Josef Stalin – they had vision but they lacked the follow through. Greed blinds, Peter my boy, don't lose sight of the goal. You won't fail me, will you?"

"This cannot fail. There is no one who can stand in my way. I have waited, I have been patient, I have served you well and we will not fail, you have my word." As he spoke, and with his head still bowed, Peter stood and backed away from Moloch, his Master. Moloch stood for the power he craved; he was fed by centuries of service and sacrifice. But Peter Nixon still believed more in himself than the god he served. He relied on no one else and ultimately he would share the supreme power he was focused on with nobody – not even the beast before him. He continued to look down, conscious that he did not want his eyes to betray him.

Little did he know that a fifteen year old boy had the potential to derail his plan. A boy not blinded by a lust for power, or an unfailing belief in his own good ideas: but a boy who had stopped; looked; and seen that all was not what it seemed.

Chapter 43: New Year

It was January the first and Xander had arranged to meet Rosie and Dan at the Castle, spurred on by a new sense of urgency to try to combat whatever it was that had invaded and corrupted the Mind Palace. As he stepped off the Elevator, he was shocked by the extent of the cloud cover. No longer was it just individual clouds in the sky above the Castle, it had become a swirling, boiling shroud of darkness, that hung ominously, emitting an atmosphere all of its own.

"Oh no!" he breathed.

"Xander, you were right!" Rosie's face was pensive, and there was a flicker of something in her eyes that he saw mirrored in Dan's: fear.

"Where's it come from?" Dan asked. "What does it mean?"

"It's not going to be good, I can tell you that much. It's been building over the last few months as whatever it is that has infiltrated the Collective has been slowly gathering pace. I believe it is the handiwork of Peter Nixon."

"He's the Prime Minister for God's sake! You can't go around making accusations like that mate; you'll end up in the Tower of London or something!"

In spite of the seriousness of what they believed themselves to be up against, they all laughed. It broke something, it released them from the stasis of fear they had felt. The other two looked at Xander; looked at him in a way they hadn't before – like he was their leader or something, possessor of the key of knowledge.

"Are we going in?" Rosie asked – sounding braver than she felt.

"Yes, we're going in!" Xander confirmed, unflinchingly.

Inside the Castle walls, it felt even more oppressive – if that were indeed possible. They headed straight for the Family Room – a room they had all spent a lot of time in and had a special affinity with. Xander's heart sank, it was almost unrecognisable as there was no light at all playing at the windows where they had been so accustomed to seeing it. There was an intense and pervading gloom accompanied by a chill which caused goose bumps to involuntarily rise up on their skin. Xander suspected it was more than the cold that initiated this instinctive response. The previously honeyed stone was dull and lifeless – that was it, he thought, the life was gone from this place. He forced himself to examine the room – although every instinct told him to get out of there. The fact that it was still here, he thought, meant that Nixon – or whoever it was – no, definitely Nixon, he decided, still had a need for it. That was when he spotted the other door, moments before it opened and a beautiful woman emerged from behind it.

"Greetings," she welcomed them, in her sing song voice. "Have you come here on behalf of your families?" It was Naamah, and it was the first encounter the three of them had had with her.

"No thank you," Xander replied, curtly, realising that it was a pretty pointless thing to say when one was standing in the Family Room. She looked surprised by his brusqueness. "Who are you, anyway?" he added, holding his nerve.

"I am Naamah, your guide to the new phase of the Collective. The old way has become corrupted and Scarlett has sent me to help you through to the new way. It is through this door. Come, let me show you." They were surprised to see this woman – no, entity seemed a better word – although she didn't appear to be dangerous in any way. She spoke so gently, so enticingly, with an almost hypnotic quality to her voice. Rosie had already been persuaded and found herself moving closer to the doorway and the captivating, beautiful woman who beckoned them when Xander spoke again, more harshly, not wanting to take any unnecessary risks.

"No. Not today. We have other things to take care of. Come on Rosie, it's time we left."

An almost imperceptible flash of irritation crossed Naamah's face, she was not used to her powers of persuasion being ineffectual – this young man needed watching, she thought. It was such a tiny reaction, that Xander wondered if he had seen it at all, but she recovered instantly and bowed her head, graciously. "As you wish," she said, and smiled. She would play the long game with these ones if necessary, but she always won in the end.

A quick investigation of the Castle rooms revealed that all of them were empty and some of the new doors stood open, but the children did not venture down any of them – it seemed a foolish risk to take at this point, unarmed with any knowledge that might be to their advantage. They saw another beautiful, white, angel-like creature talking to a group of children out in the courtyard when they went back outside, but the Throne Room had been empty and there was no sign of Scarlett, or Peter Nixon for that matter.

"Have you got her mobile number?" Dan asked, obviously picking up on the potential danger of the situation.

"Yes, for emergencies," Xander replied.

"I think this qualifies as one, don't you?"

Chapter 44: Scarlett

Xander contacted Scarlett straight away, as soon as he got back to his room. The three of them had decided they would all go together – partly to provide a united front to support Scarlett and also because, well, try and stop any of them from being there; they were as committed as each other to the Collective. It was unusual for them to have to meet in Scarlett's office – normally they could convene in the Castle if they wanted an emergency forum, but the fact that the Castle **was** the problem, meant that the way they would normally operate was now out of the question. They had some tough issues to discuss with Scarlett – the time for diplomacy had come to an end - they would need to make some difficult decisions about the future and it was best for them to be in one place to do that – even though it took a bit longer to physically get everyone together. Fortunately they were all based in London, so logistically it wasn't a complete nightmare, just strange to be going back and doing it 'old school' as it were.

"Have you seen it?" Rosie asked, once they were all sat on the crimson sofas in Scarlett's office. There was no time for small talk, and frankly, nobody had the least inclination to engage in it.

"Yes," she replied quietly, knowing exactly to what they were referring. She had been to the Castle earlier on that day and was still reeling from the abomination that had greeted her. They had all been shocked by her appearance when they had arrived at the office. She looked like a broken woman and about ten years older than the Scarlett they were used to seeing. "I can't believe it. I just can't." She looked small and vulnerable as she sat there, twisting her hands together in her lap and staring at a fleck of lint on the carpeted floor. It was as if there had been a role reversal and Xander found himself to be the one who took charge of the situation.

"You've got to get a grip Scarlett," he said, firmly but with compassion. "This is serious and it's intensifying by the day. Do you have any idea what might be behind it?"

"Well, obviously somebody has hijacked it somehow. I can't think of another reason. The Brightness itself would not have turned against us, so somebody has interfered with it. It was meant to be the solution, not just another problem. The world is full of good ideas which haven't quite worked; I just didn't see this being one of them."

"There's no time to have a pity party. Do you have a back-up plan? Is there any way of undoing what's been done?" Xander did not want to be harsh with her, but he knew he had to get her focused on how to move forwards. He had to engage the forthright, matter-of-fact Scarlett who knew what to do and when to do it.

"I didn't foresee this; call me naïve, but I believed that once people saw the potential of the Collective they would get behind it. Why would anyone want to derail something that was making such progress in terms of community transformation? It didn't occur to me that it would be corrupted. Our nation was crying out for something like this. I can't believe that we've had our chance and failed." Although it was a statement of how she felt, she addressed it like a question and Xander felt her pain and hopelessness.

"Can you think of anyone who might have an agenda here? Or was there any point in the development of the Collective that you found yourself making a decision that didn't quite sit right – something questionable? Does anything come to mind; anything at all?" Dan asked this question and he could feel Xander's eyes burning into him, although he didn't look directly at him to confirm it. He wanted to offer an alternative to Scarlett to the theory he knew Xander was going to propose at any instant – which even now, at this desperate moment, he hoped beyond all hope was wrong. Surely it was exceeding the realms of possibility that the Prime Minister, former Education Minister, supporter of the Collective right from the early days, facilitator of its introduction to schools, could be the orchestrator of its downfall?

"I can't think of anyone, Dan, no. Everyone has been so positive, so helpful." She paused for a moment and Xander thought he saw her mentally taking a closer look at some little incident that had occurred and lodged in her memory, before discarding it.

"What is it?" he asked, leaning forward and engaging her with eye contact, hoping he could encourage her to voice whatever it was that had flitted across her consciousness. But she had clouded over again, he could see her sink back into despair. Scarlett was normally so perceptive, that was what frustrated him so much about all of this. Why was this such a mental stumbling block for her? Why hadn't she seen it, felt it, as quickly and as keenly as he did? Was it pride? Arrogance? Confusion? Or just a blind spot, created when one has complete faith in something which one hasn't been able to stand back and view with objectivity?

"No, it's nothing," she remarked finally. But as she spoke, it was as if the thought insinuated itself upon her mind once again and a flicker of recognition passed across her face. Xander decided not to push her. The seed had been sown, he would gain nothing from pressurising her and maybe alienating her. The best course of action, he decided, was to let it germinate and root itself in a place where she would not be able to ignore it. If he was right about Nixon – and he was almost one hundred percent confident that he was – then he was sure that eventually Scarlett would see it too. How long did they have though? It was one of the toughest decisions he had ever had to make, but he knew he was doing the right thing.

"Leave it with me," she said decisively. Already he perceived a shift; she had regained some of her usual aura of control. He smiled at her, his eyes shouting, 'I believe in you. We need you. You can do this!'

"I'll come up with something," she said, standing up and smoothing an imaginary wrinkle from the front of her dress. She was back!

Chapter 45: The Broadcast

It was strange not being able to go to the Castle, or having the regular contact with Scarlett that he had become accustomed to. Xander had tried texting Scarlett, just to make sure she was alright – their meeting had been hard on her, he realised, but it had to be said and he was encouraged by the way she had rallied by the end of it. He was hopeful that she would come up with something – she was the creator of the Castle after all, if anyone could do it, she could. She had not replied to his text – he was disappointed, but not discouraged. She needed time, he understood, time to herself to regain her composure and her fight, and time to work on the solution. Therefore, when a message was passed around school three days after their meeting, inviting all members of the Collective to go to room 102, Xander was as much in the dark as any of them as to what the meeting was about. He met up with Rosie on the way there.

"Do you know what this is concerning? Is it Scarlett summoning us, or someone else?"

"I have no idea," Xander replied, truthfully. "She hasn't responded to my message, so I left her alone. It could be good news," there was an echo of uncertainty in his voice. He heard it himself, although he was trying to be positive for Rosie's benefit. Was it a niggle of doubt, or was it just that he felt a little bit aggrieved that if it was Scarlett, she hadn't run anything by them – him, he admitted to himself that it was personal. He shrugged it off, annoyed with himself that he still felt this need for approval and to be valued within the elite group that governed the Collective. At times like this, Xander felt older than his years and wistful for the time when he was an ordinary boy, doing ordinary things. But he could not deny that he felt the weight of responsibility for this movement; a burden of authority that went beyond wishful thinking. He was carrying something on behalf of the Collective, its DNA or something, he couldn't explain it he just knew he could not walk away. There were times when he imagined the Brightness itself was calling to him to come and find it, to make everything right again.

They arrived at the small tutorial room which contained a round table that could seat about ten people at a push. Fortunately they were a small group within school – a couple more had joined the Collective over the last year, influenced by the changes that had taken place. Sometimes Xander was a little disappointed by the lack of numbers of followers within his school and community, but at times like this he remembered the wise words of a friend of Scarlett's:

"How many people does it take to turn a town? Fewer than you think!"

He looked around at the eager faces. There was a laptop on the table set to play some kind of media message. They sat down, placing the laptop in such a position that everyone could see the screen.

"What's this about, Xander?" one of the other children asked. "Is it because the windows aren't letting in light anymore? I tried to visualise something for my family yesterday and I didn't get anywhere!"

"I know! What's the problem? It must be those clouds. There was a woman there, she looked like an angel or something, she told me they were building some new rooms to help us," another one added.

"That's what I heard, too."

"I dunno what's going on. We need to settle down and watch this media clip. Maybe Scarlett has thought of something and things can go back to the way they were." Xander took charge of the group, anxious to find out what was on the clip. "Okay?" he asked, looking up around the table at his peers. They nodded in unison and he selected the play icon. Suddenly the screen came to life and there was Scarlett, in her trademark red suit dress. Xander realised, as he exhaled with relief, that he had been holding his breath.

"Thank you all for your attendance. I wanted to speak to everyone, so I arranged for your schools to gather you together and play this message because I want you all to know about the recent developments in the Castle. Some of you have been alarmed by the cloud formation and the lack of the Brightness within the rooms which seems to be interfering with our visualisations. I did not foresee this development when I designed the Castle, I can only assume it is some kind of glitch in the original blueprint. I am keen for us to keep operating as so much has been achieved over the last year, so I have made some modifications to the Castle by way of new doorways that lead to secondary rooms. It seemed easier to adapt the original structure, as you are all familiar with accessing the Castle through the Elevator. Restructuring everything would have been far too time consuming and involved, and particularly in these difficult times, it was important for me to get you guys back in to the Castle and operating as soon as possible so we can get things back on track. The new rooms do not rely on the Brightness that we were used to using in the original Castle rooms, but we now have guides who have come to help us. They are light-bearers and they will take you to the new rooms – exactly as before, go to the room which best fits your needs and await their guidance. These light-bearers will then provide the light necessary for visualisation as the windows used to do – just focus on them instead of the window and extract power from them as you used to filter it from the Brightness. The beauty of this is they can join in with you to make your visualisation all the more powerful as you draw energy from them and allow them to assist you. We will overcome these problems together, do not be alarmed – and certainly do not avoid the Castle, there is nothing to fear, I assure you. What this does give us is a thrilling opportunity however, for a new way of doing things. This is a new era for the Castle, exciting times lie ahead. Thank you for your attention. Please visit the Castle again as soon as you can and continue with your work under the new system, it is vital that we keep going. I look forward to seeing you there soon." The clip came to an abrupt end and the screen went blank.

Xander stared at it in disbelief. This was the very last thing he had expected Scarlett to say. Rosie, on the other hand, looked relieved and happy with the outcome. "I thought that angel woman was okay. See, you worry too much!"

Xander was not as easily convinced. "It doesn't add up, Rosie. Why would Scarlett not mention this to us the other day? We saw her after we saw the guide in the Castle."

"We didn't talk about it though, did we. She might not have know we had seen one. Besides, she might have only just realised how useful they are," Rosie stated, with her usual positivity and optimism. "I think they have come to help us. A physical form of the Brightness, if you like."

"I want to talk to Scarlett about it face-to-face first. I still have some questions."

Rosie rolled her eyes, "Okay, Mr Excessive! Whatever you want."

"I'll catch you later, I just need a bit of time to myself," Xander said, as he left the bustling room where everyone seemed to have started talking together and none of it made any sense. Something about this wasn't right, but why had Scarlett gone along with it? She looked so bright and breezy, so different from how she had appeared only three days ago when the weight of the world seemed to rest on her shoulders. Why the change of tack, what was she playing at? Could she be trusted after all? He hated that he had even asked himself this last question. He must talk to her as soon as was humanly possible. Without looking back, or questioning the ethics of the decision he had just made, Xander illicitly left the school campus and headed for Scarlett's office. No time like the present, he thought, grimly.

Chapter 46: Warning

Rosie looked at the door which Xander had just left through, feeling a little abandoned, yet determined to see the positives in what had just occurred. Due to the high volume of chatter in the room, she would have missed the 'ping' of the text message on her phone if it hadn't vibrated in her pocket. She took it out and opened the message:

'Hi Rosie, it's Lucie, you helped me out a few weeks ago. I need to talk to someone . . . urgently. Didn't know who else to turn to. It's about the broadcast. It's not good news. Can we meet?'

Rosie was puzzled by the text, but she felt the exigency of the request. The most obvious place to meet was in the Castle – Lucie could be from anywhere in the country, this was still the most convenient place to assemble. But she didn't want to do this without Xander. She left the room, looking for somewhere quiet, and called Xander as she went.

"Hi Xander," she spoke in to her handset, annoyed it had gone to voice mail. "It's me. I just got a message from that girl Lucie, the one you gave my number to. She said there was something wrong with the broadcast and she wants to meet, urgently. I am going to suggest going to the Castle, as I don't know where she's from. I would really appreciate it if you could come too, I don't want to do this on my own. Where are you, by the way? Call me, or just get straight to the Castle, soon as you can." She hung up, praying he would get her message promptly and join her. Something squirmed in her stomach where a few minutes ago calm and relief had been. Xander was right, again, and she was too trusting. She chastised herself as she went off to the room they used routinely for access to the Castle. As she went, she replied to Lucie's text:

'On my way to the Castle. Meet there ASAP. Stay outside. Have asked Xander to come too. Rosie.'

It was brief but persuasive, and she felt sure Lucie would be there, but would Xander? She was a little afraid, realising just how much she had come to rely on him. But she could do this, she convinced herself, she had to.

When Rosie exited the Elevator, a slight, plain looking girl was already standing there, looking worried. Lucie, she assumed – although there was no sign of Xander.

"Hi, thanks so much for coming," the girl said, nervously looking over her shoulder at the Castle. "We don't have to go in there, do we?"

"No," Rosie reassured her, "I think it's best if we talk out here. Now, tell me what's happened. What are you afraid of?"

Xander had taken the tube straight to Scarlett's building. In his mind, he saw himself walking directly in to her office to confront her about what was going on. Unfortunately, we cannot predict what will happen in real life, and when Xander arrived and walked over to Scarlett's receptionist, he was both shocked and disappointed to find that she wasn't there.

"When will she be back?" he asked, unable to keep the frustration from his voice.

"I don't know, she left in a hurry."

"I'll wait," he said, turning to the chair he had occupied only a few weeks before, when the pressure of all of this had just started to build. Little did he know then that it would escalate so quickly and with such devastation. He took out his phone and noticed a missed call from Rosie. He listened to her message, then jumped up and rushed over to Jess. "Can I use her office? This is urgent, I need to get to the Castle!"

"I don't see why not," she said, looking a bit reluctant. "Just don't touch anything!"

Xander entered, closed the door and glanced at the swivel chair in front of the desk with a touch of the green-eyed monster. He couldn't do it. He sat on the sofa instead and composed himself for a trip up to the Castle.

He emerged from the Elevator to find Rosie deep in conversation with a girl he recognised as Lucie. They were walking around, but in no particular direction. "Rosie!" he shouted.

She turned, registered it was him and smiled with relief. "Thank goodness you're here! You've got to listen to this." Turning to Lucie she said, "Can you tell Xander what you told me?"

She nodded and looked at the tall, handsome, confident boy who was walking towards them. "I didn't know who to turn to, who I could trust, but I remembered you and Rosie. You are really respected in the Collective. Something happened to me a few weeks ago, it scared me. I thought it would be better to stay away . . "

"Just back up a minute, Lucie. What's this all about?" Xander felt, on some subconscious level which he couldn't quite understand or account for, that Lucie had something vital to share that would shed light on what was going on and help them to understand it.

"I saw Scarlett's broadcast earlier and I knew I had to say something. I don't think that was her!"

"What do you mean, not her?" Xander was incredulous, but Rosie touched his arm and hushed him with her eyes.

"Let her explain."

"A couple of months ago, I had a visit from a woman called Naamah in a dream. She told me things; knew things about my mother. She said she could take me to her – my mother died when I was younger." She paused, not for sympathy – she had had quite enough of that – but to collect her thoughts. Rosie squeezed her shoulder, comfortingly. "She told me to meet her in the Castle and took me through a special door round behind the keep, to a room with my mother in it. Well, I thought it was my mum – perhaps I was just desperate for it to be my mum and I think that's what they were banking on – but now I'm not so sure. I think I was being manipulated. Basically, they . . "

"Sorry Lucie, but that's the second time you have said 'they'. Who do you mean by that?" Xander asked, intently.

"Let her finish, Xander!" Rosie said, sharply. "Carry on," she reassured Lucie, with a smile.

"Well, they got me to bring this boy, Jack – the one I asked you about Rosie. I'm sorry I used you in this, but I didn't realise what I was involved in. I wish I hadn't done it now, but I wanted to see my mum, and . . . ." Lucie started to cry.

Rosie hugged her. "Take your time, Lucie. I know this is hard for you, but you are doing great, believe me."

Xander was impatient to hear the details, but he managed to hold his tongue, not wanting to incur further wrath from Rosie. He clenched his fists and walked in a brief, tight circle staring down at his feet as he waited for them to finish their touchy feely thing - which girls seem so good at and boys find pointless!

"I took Jack with me and we were taken down a corridor to a different room. Peter Nixon was there."

"I knew it!" Xander exploded, his head snapping up, making poor Lucie jump. "What did he do?" His eyes flashed with anger and contempt for this man who had raised his hackles right from the start and proved himself to be the devious, scheming low-life that Xander had him pegged as – stooping to the depths of manipulating this poor girl through her dead mother. He hated him!

"He told Jack that his dad was in danger from a terror attack. Practically encouraged him to visualise the explosion in the House of Commons. I was there, but we didn't know what was happening; didn't know the power of our words! I promise, we didn't know! I couldn't believe it when I saw the news!" Her tears fell afresh. "I swear, we thought all we were doing was calling for policy change and a cabinet reshuffle, no one was more shocked . . ." her voice trailed off.

"Nobody blames you, Lucie. He's the one who's culpable for this, not you! Do you know what he's up to?"

"I don't know, but those light people are working for him, I just know it. And another thing; they've got some kind of shape shifter or something working for them – I think that's how they pretended to be my mum. And the maintenance guy? The one they couldn't find? I'm sure that was him too! That broadcast today confirmed it for me, I really don't think that was Scarlett."

"What? How is that possible?" Rosie was incredulous. Lucie hadn't got that far in her account earlier, this was the first she had heard of the accusation about a shape shifter. But, horrific as it was to try to comprehend, it had the ring of truth to it.

"I'm telling you, I don't understand all this stuff, or what power they are drawing from – it's pretty sinister and way bigger than I thought."

"It makes sense," Xander said, nodding - much to Lucie's relief - as little pieces of the puzzle started to slot into place in his mind. "What about Jack?"

"I don't know. I can't get hold of him, he's changed his number." Lucie shrugged, helplessly.

"I told you it was weird, Scarlett saying all that stuff. We have to talk to her. I was at her office when I got your message, but she wasn't there. Fancy going there now, to wait for her?"

"I can't really, I live in Dorset," Lucie said.

"It's okay," Rosie added, "We'll go and see her and explain everything you have told us. If she wants to talk to you, I'll text you and you can meet us here. Is that okay?"

As they finished up their conversation, they realised more and more young people were arriving and heading for the Castle. The broadcast had obviously had the desired effect, and those who had stayed away, uneasy about the recent conditions, were coming back under the assurance of the one they believed in.

"There isn't much time," Xander urged. "Who knows what that evil sicko will do next?" They left the realm of the imagination and headed back to the real one – Lucie back to Dorset and Xander and Rosie to a show down in Scarlett's office.

Chapter 47: Take Over

Peter Nixon stood in the Throne Room of the Castle. It was very different from how it had been designed, with a deep and penetrating gloom. The windows encircling the room stood lifeless and grey. Where previously a myriad of variegated colours, like some trip induced hallucination, had danced playfully, now there was nothing. He looked around at the empty circular table and abandoned swivel chairs that stood at odd angles to one another in a careless fashion. "You've had your day, Miss Tang," he almost growled, gleefully. "Now it's mine!" He grabbed the back of the nearest chair and spun it, disrespectfully, then turned to the staircase and descended, slowly, down through the aperture in the floor.

Nixon was delighted with the response they had had to the broadcast – Scarlett still had her uses. It would not be easy to keep exploiting her like this, she was bound to get wind of what he was doing, but she still engendered a remarkable amount of trust and respect where the children were concerned. He would need to find a strategy to keep her out of the way, he thought to himself. It shouldn't be too difficult for someone of his calibre. One step at a time though, he was keen to consolidate what had been so recently established. Children were, as he had predicted, coming back to the Castle in droves and – thanks to his endorsement of them, on behalf of the lovely Scarlett – they were also responding well to the guides. This part had gone better than he had predicted. He had anticipated a little more resistance from them, assuming they would be more wary of the guides. But Naamah, particularly, had served him well. She was so beautiful, so beguiling, who could resist her feminine charms and gloriously radiant appearance? Nobody, it seemed. He smiled to himself as he thought of the faceless, grey being that skulked behind the resplendent façade, and afforded himself a chuckle of rapturous delight.

It was true, the guides had done a splendid job of ushering the ignorant children, gently and with encouragement, through the new doors and in to the alternative rooms. They were marvellous at artifice, for they had a way of distracting the children from the cold, hardness of the rooms they entered by dazzling them with their own light. The young people were used to focusing on the Brightness and using it to form and see their visualisations, so it was a straightforward transition for them to concentrate their attention on the light of the guides instead. It was a master stroke and Nixon sensed that Moloch was pleased with his offering. With the children unwittingly channelling their visualisations through his guides, they could be manipulated and coerced to do his bidding. He thought of the two weak-minded individuals who had helped him get this far and gave a snort of distain. He had no time for people who cared so much for others that they were willing to jeopardise themselves. Relationships created a point of weakness and this was a trap he did not intend to fall in to; ever. His parents had done him a favour, he thought, abandoning him. It had taught him to rely on the only person you could trust – yourself. He believed in no one or nothing with the same ferocity and loyalty as he believed in himself – Peter Michael Nixon. Even his initials prophesied his success, his destiny. He would have what he wanted – control, power, worship even. As he became known among the nations, Moloch would once again be enthroned in the high places and nothing would stop them.

Where Scarlett had brought unity and a common desire to improve society, Nixon would bring discord and fear – turning people against their neighbours, their colleagues, their families; forcing them to compete and mistrust to survive. People retreat in to themselves at such times, when they are faced with an emergency situation, and the compulsion to survive kicks in. This base instinct strips back centuries of civilization and causes people to revert to an almost animal urge to look after number one. He had managed, in a ridiculously short space of time, to gain governmental control of the country and this had put him in the position where he not only had the ability to dictate certain laws and conditions, he was actually trusted and heralded as the one to take them out of the place they now found themselves in. Ironically, Scarlett had probably helped him to achieve the possibility of instigating even more extreme measures because of the contrast between what had been and what was now. People had let their guard down, started to believe in and trust something better. Nothing makes the heart sicker than disappointment, so they were all the more willing to accept his severe measures because they were afraid of being caught out again, afraid of hoping for more and seeing those hopes dashed. He had financial control too and would soon be in a position to track the movements of citizens and see the paper trail of their transactions to the minutest detail. This would further allow for manipulation and control as he would put the banks and businesses in charge of targeting people based on their history of financial decision making. He took pleasure from all of this, but he took the most delight in the prospect of controlling the children and dismantling the whole notion of family. A hot flash burnt through him; anger – what had family ever done for him? He brought it under control - anger was dangerous, it led to weak choices - he would not let it sidetrack him. The past was the past, it had made him who he was and he would not allow a moment of self pity to influence him. He would continue with his restrictions on freedom – how gullible people were! He loved the simplicity of it, yet it was genius – the simplest things often were. This disaster had been entirely of his own making so he could implement the solution – and be heralded as the saviour of the people along the way!

On his way down the stairs, Peter Nixon greeted and encouraged the young people coming up. "Glad you came back, we need you . . . Welcome, find your room, the guides will help you . . . Thank you for returning to serve the Collective, you've done the right thing . . ." Brilliant! He basked in the success of his plan, feeling the intoxicating and heady effect of it filling his being and energising him. He saw the path ahead with intense clarity and was delighted that he had succeeded with such completeness. He continued to welcome the eager young minds who had come to re-engage with the new dawn of the Collective whilst simultaneously, they blindly entered in to a pact with the Devil.

Chapter 48: Would the Real Scarlett Tang . . .

Scarlett answered her phone on the first ring. "Xander, hi. What's up?" She sounded distracted to him.

"We need to talk, where are you?"

"I had a strange call to meet with one of the members of the Inner Circle about a matter of some urgency. But when I arrived at their office, they were nowhere to be seen. Very odd. I'm just on my way back now."

Xander was not surprised that she had been sent on some wild goose chase, probably to get her out of the way so there was no chance of her coming to the Castle and upsetting Nixon's carefully orchestrated little plan! "Not so very odd I'm afraid, I'll explain when I see you. Better not talk over the phone, don't know who's listening. Can Rosie and I come to your office?"

"What, now? Shouldn't you two be in school?"

"This is urgent. I'm already here actually, and Rosie's on her way. See you shortly." Xander hung up the phone and looked round the office. It had only just occurred to him that it might not be safe to talk on the phone, but what if Scarlett's office had been bugged or something? He checked himself, laughing hollowly at his own paranoia. How had it come to this? What kind of a world was he living in when he started to worry about the cloak and dagger antics of a megalomaniac of a politician! It did not comfort him though. The thought only grew in to something sinister, black and fear inducing. He felt his own isolation in that moment intensely. Felt the creeping fingers of dread advance up his spine, leaving him clammy and agitated. He knew nothing of supernatural things, he had not even really thought about the spiritual nature of what it was he had been engaged in over the last year – it had just felt so natural, so easy and so right that he had not questioned what it was that drove it. But in that moment, he knew he was engaged in something much more powerful and much less visible than a physical war, or the recognition of character flaws or falseness. This was about something evil encroaching on him and the ones he knew and loved. This was more than one man's misguided attempt at ruling over a nation. He shuddered at the knowledge of what they were up against and wondered what Scarlett herself knew.

When the door opened and Scarlett walked in, Xander realised he had been pacing the room. He stopped and looked at her. She must have seen it – the fear – because her expression changed from one that was all set for a greeting to a more stricken countenance.

"What is it?" she asked, in a small voice.

"I'm scared, Scarlett. I'm scared. What have we got involved in?"

"What do you mean?" Her expression changed to concern and she walked swiftly over to him and instinctively stroked his right arm in a gesture of comfort, seeing the boy he was for the first time almost. Her heart went out to him. "Talk to me."

""Why did you decide to operate from the Castle, Scarlett? What took you to that realm in the first place?"

She looked surprised by his question, then wistful. "It seemed to draw me to it. My heart was open to change, I wanted to lead people to find their identities, to believe in a better way and it sort of found me; showed me what to do. I can't explain it any better I'm afraid."

"What ever it was, I always saw it as a good thing, did you?"

"Of course I did," she urged, looking intensely at him. "I still believe in it!"

"I think there is an opposite force at work here now, something evil that has worked its way in and taken over. Does that sound mad to you?"

"No, it doesn't." She shook her head and looked down at the floor. Her beautiful hair fell across her face and he thought he heard her crying. He stood, awkwardly, waiting for her to speak. Suddenly, the door opened and Rosie walked in. "We'll sort this," Scarlett said, quietly, looking him straight in the eye. He looked at her tear streaked face, he had never believed in her more.

Wiping her cheek briskly, Scarlett walked over to her desk, keeping her back to them both as she composed herself. "So," she said, trying to sound breezy, "what's this about?"

"The broadcast!" Xander and Rosie both said in unison.

"What broadcast?" Scarlett looked puzzled. She turned her gaze on Xander, virtually ignoring Rosie, so he spoke.

"Earlier today, we were summoned together to hear a broadcast, supposedly from you, about the new rooms . . ."

"Wait, I haven't done any broadcast!" Scarlett interrupted, fiercely.

"I know, it's okay, we know it wasn't you," and Xander went on to explain what was contained in the transmission to schools – which horrified her – then Lucie's revelations about what had happened with Nixon and Jack – which shocked her to the very core.

For a long time she remained silent, then quietly she assented, "You were right!"

"This isn't about being right, Scarlett, for God's sake! This is serious. Nixon has some kind of plan for world domination or something and he's operating out of the Castle and has adapted it to suit whatever power it is he is drawing on; whatever evil collaboration he is working with. We are not just dealing with the man, that's what I was trying to tell you before. How do we fight this thing, Scarlett? What do we do?"

Xander felt desperate. He knew he sounded crazy, paranoid and overly dramatic. But he also knew that he wasn't very far from the truth.

"What have you been doing for the last three days, anyway?" He was angry now, but he couldn't stop himself. "While Nixon's been building his empire, what have you been doing? Have you come up with anything to save the Collective?"

"I have an idea, yes," she said, looking defiantly at Xander. He felt guilty for speaking so harshly to her. "But first I have to go to the Castle and warn the children. They need to know whatever it is Nixon is using – a shape shifter you say? – that it's not me. How I do that, I have no idea! But are you coming?" She may have been small, but Scarlett Tang on the warpath was a fearsome thing to behold.

Chapter 49: Hopeless

It felt even worse than he remembered, just from that morning. They were all shocked as they alighted from the Elevator – it seemed as though almost all of the natural light had been extinguished by the clouds and the warmth along with it. A chill wind was blowing across the plain which separated them from the Castle, whipping up the sand and sending it, spitefully, in to their eyes and on any exposed areas of skin. Xander held up his hand to shelter his eyes, squinting against the dust storm, and looked at Scarlett.

She just stood there, staring. "Why would he do this?" she asked, desperately. "This was my life's work, my dream. It was a good dream too, I don't understand. People benefited from it. You benefited from it!" She turned on them, almost vehemently.

"We're on your side, you know," Xander reassured her, trying to ignore the shock and hurt he felt from her accusatory words.

"I know. . . . . I'm sorry. I'm glad you two are here." She smiled weakly at them.

"Come on," Rosie urged Scarlett, gently. Xander was touched by her tenderness, she was such a deeply compassionate person. She always seemed able to tune in to people's feelings and engage them. Xander could read situations, motives, things like that, but Rosie had a gift for reaching out and comforting people. He smiled at her over Scarlett's head; they were a good team.

Fundamentally, the Castle looked the same as it always had – imposing and solid – but it could not have felt more different. The light and temperature were more than atmospheric conditions, even they felt intimidating and malevolent. The warm stone had lost its lustrous honey glow and just looked hard and unforgiving. At that moment, Xander realised it was the people and the driving force behind something that affected it and made it what it was; the structure itself – which he had always marvelled at and felt had something magical about it – was only a building. It was a stark lesson to learn, whether to put your trust in bricks and mortar or people. He chose people. They let you down, they messed things up, they misunderstood you, but ultimately that's what it was all about. For this reason, he could not accept what was happening to the hundreds of children inside this organisation. They deserved to know what was going on, they deserved better than Peter Nixon, they needed the truth – and it was up to them to find a way of turning this around. As they walked under the arch way in to the courtyard – as he had so many times before, albeit with a completely different agenda – Xander resolved to find a way to make this right; with or without Scarlett. He would see what she came up with first – perhaps she could handle it, after all – but if she failed he would take it on.

They had hoped to see children in the courtyard, or on the staircase as they made their way up to the Throne Room, but the Castle appeared to be empty. He didn't know what Scarlett had been expecting – maybe to just walk in there, meet a few kids and say, "Hey guys, it's me. I'm the real Scarlett, don't listen to the other one, she works for Peter Nixon as some kind of shape shifter. Tell your friends, this is all a big ruse to get you to serve him." It sounded like nonsense, even to Xander who knew the truth. He had no idea how they were going to pull this off and the more they walked around, looking into empty room after empty room, the more he knew that this was not the answer.

"Come on Scarlett, this isn't going to help. It was a mistake to come here."

"I can't go yet, I need to see the Throne Room."

"Why? It's over. This phase of things is over, you have to accept that."

"I can't! Not yet!" She was crying and his heart went out to her. "I need to know if anyone else from the Inner Circle is here." He could understand why she wanted to do this. She needed to know the extent of the betrayal.

Scarlett felt more than just the treachery of her so called friends, she was jealous too, and it surprised her. Peter had taken what was hers and she felt like behaving like a spoilt child. It wasn't fair! None of this was. But it was the truth; reality in this jumbled up mess that had become her life. It had taken her slightly longer to realise it, but Scarlett was now on the same page as Xander – this problem was not going to be solved here, it was too late for that. There was no point in rushing in to one of the new rooms to bluster about like lunatics, this was Peter Nixon's kingdom now. It was pretty obvious in the light of what he was doing to the country and what he had done here, that Peter Nixon was not a man to be reasoned with. He would have found a way to cement people's faith in him and their approach would need to be more subtle, more clandestine.

"Time to go," Scarlett said firmly. Xander's heart skipped a beat and in the midst of the disappointment and hopelessness of the situation they had found themselves in, he felt something rise up within him. . . . . "I do have an idea, and being here has confirmed to me that it's probably our best chance. It's wild and untried, but it just might work."

. . . . It was hope.

Chapter 50: Portals

"I like it," Xander said, when they were back in Scarlett's office. "But where are you going to put it so Nixon doesn't notice?"

"That's true," Rosie added, looking perturbed. "He'll shut it down somehow if he finds it."

"I'm going to locate the permanent side here in my office. I've used portals a couple of times when I was developing the Castle, but I've never tried to create one. It may take some time, but if it works then I'm hoping we can use it to travel back and undo some of the things Nixon has done. My main concern is that we can't draw attention to ourselves, which means that what we can do, will be fairly peripheral. I'm concerned we won't be able to do anything too radical as it will get noticed and that will be that. Either we work slowly and purposefully, undermining things there subtly while we build momentum, or we go for an all out blast of action and literally risk everything."

"At the moment, I don't think we have a choice. We have to go subtle until we see what kind of results we are getting. 'Slowly, slowly, catchy monkey', isn't that what they say?"

"Or catchy sick evil weirdo! Doesn't have quite the same ring to it, but it's probably a more accurate description!" Rosie rarely said anything critical about people, but she said this with passion, laced with humour, and Xander smiled.

"Bravo!" he congratulated, warmly. "Let's stop him, whatever it takes!"

"Whatever it takes," Scarlett repeated, looking more hopeful and stronger than she had for days. "Can you give me some time? I'll text you both when I'm ready."

"Of course," Xander said. "Good luck."

Scarlett had explored other realms quite extensively when she was developing the mind Castle. She had seen others travelling through and operating in those realms too. Her first experience had been using a portal to explore planes in the spirit realm. During a meditation time, she had had an open vision, in which a stone gothic-style arch had appeared before her. It had looked inviting and she had walked towards it. The strange thing was, that as she walked through it, she had found herself in an other-worldly place. It was a garden like none she had seen before, where the colours were vibrant and alive; where flowers behaved like butterflies and water made beautiful music all of its own. People walked in the garden, they smiled at her with glowing, friendly faces, but said not a word. It was the most alluring place she had ever been and it inspired her to create an area which could be visited and used to initiate her utopian ideal. She received knowledge about this place that seemed to be downloaded into her mind directly. She was told it was called Ma'on, the residence of ministering angels. She loved it and would visit it from time to time, coming away refreshed.

Essentially, the Elevator itself was a portal into this realm, just a different dimension of it. She had travelled in several alternative levels within this realm – there were said to be seven realms, but she had not visited them all. One of the levels was called Machon, it was reputedly the source of harmful phenomena and Scarlett had thought about it several times over the past few weeks, wondering if Nixon had somehow managed to pollute the Castle by drawing the Machon into it. She did not know how on earth she could undo something like this – she firmly suspected that he had the assistance of some malevolent force, because it was not humanly possible to corrupt these levels in any natural way. She did not think that a portal purely for inter-dimensional travel would be the solution here, as, if the boundaries had become blurred, any interference on her part could well be detected by her foe. Therefore, she believed that a time portal would be the thing to really assist them at this point, as it would afford them the possibility of travelling on a different plane. It was a complex structure, where the spiritual realms ran one way and were bisected by time, which – although not a linear thing, as in our limited Western perceptions – ran along a different plane. Scarlett believed there was the potential to connect the two dimensions through time – drawing together the realm where they had operated with so much success, to the world they now frustratingly inhabited.

Everything which Scarlett knew about these dimensions was what she had researched and experienced for herself. She was used to operating on her own, so when it came to developing this, she had no one specific to turn to for help with the process itself. She was a woman of immense determination and resourcefulness and she was resolved to make this work. It was only a matter of weeks before, having literally shut herself away and lived and breathed these dimensions, she finally had something which she was willing to reveal to her closest and most trusted friends. Scarlett had found that there were still people, other than Xander and Rosie, who were supportive of her and were disconcerted – to say the least – by Nixon's modus operandi. It was blissful to her to be able to return, once again, to the Castle in its natural state through the new portal. She had to force herself to share it, damaged as she had been by the betrayal of Peter Nixon and people like him. But she knew that the success of this new development depended very much on team work. She could not – and should not – do this on her own. So Scarlett Tang called a meeting.

Chapter 51: The Way Forward . . . or Back!

Xander and Rosie had waited for this moment. It had been a difficult time, watching things continue to fall apart around them on a national, local and personal level and being absolutely powerless to do anything about it. There was no point in visiting the Castle as they could not operate within it without partnering with Nixon's guides – and, as attractive as they appeared to be, they knew this was definitely not an option. So they waited. They heard nothing from Scarlett for over four weeks, but she had asked for time. As hard as it was not to pick up the phone and call or text for a progress report, or any kind of word of assurance or encouragement, they had to leave it and trust her; respect the barrier she had temporarily erected, believing at some point it would come down. So it had been with immense relief that they received the summons to her office. The limbo, they hoped, was over and they could finally get back into the battle, as it were.

It was an interesting collection of people of all ages – Lucie was there, much to their delight. Xander had suggested she be invited when he received the message about the meeting, assuring Scarlett that she could be trusted. Lucie was responsible for blowing the lid on what Nixon was up to, confirming his role in it all. To Xander, that made her a hero! There were two other members from the original Inner Circle, Xander recognised them from the early days of the Collective and assumed they were Scarlett's old college friends who had been with her from the beginning.

"Thank you all for coming," Scarlett said, by way of introduction. "I know you are all aware of the seriousness of the situation. I have called you here to reveal my latest creation and to discuss how we are to best proceed with things. You are all aware by now that the person behind the corruption of the Collective is Peter Nixon. It is my belief that he has found a way to integrate two of the spiritual realms – the one we were originally operating in which was benign and positive, with one which is evil and purely concerned with retribution and inflicting harm. He can only have done this by drawing on some demonic force – I believe he is serving a malevolent god and they have combined forces to increase their own personal power. This means, as you have probably worked out already, that we are not just up against a natural enemy in the man Peter Nixon, we are fighting an unseen and extremely powerful one simultaneously. Our challenge is to try to redeem what has been lost, in terms of the Castle, without alerting either of them as to what we are doing. Keeping things secret from Nixon would be relatively easy if it were only this natural element we were dealing with. But he seems to have these guides, overseers of the spirit realm he has connected in to the Castle and they detect any movement there with the same degree of pinpoint accuracy as a spider detects the tiniest vibrations on her web."

"So how do you propose we do that then, without being spotted?" It was Dan. As one of the old school recruits he had been invited too, and Xander was pleased to see his familiar face.

"I have developed a portal. I tested it and was able to go back to the Castle as it was in the early days." She looked wistful for a moment and everyone present found themselves, for a split second, back in the Castle with the light and warmth they had come to associate with it. "I'll grant you, it is not going to be easy to go back and undo what Peter has been doing without him noticing. We could probably not touch upon anything which he has influenced personally, because any change to his past would have repercussions in the present and he would definitely pick up on that. Also, we have his guides to contend with. I think we need to be particularly aware that the shape shifter character has the potential to infiltrate us – both in the spirit realm and in the natural. Lucie thinks he was responsible for impersonating the workman who planted the bomb in the Commons." Everyone turned to Lucie, who blushed and looked down at the table, awkwardly. "Good job," Scarlett congratulated her, and she smiled, coyly. "My best case scenario involves us operating on the periphery, picking off individuals and resetting certain situations in the hope that he is too preoccupied – and frankly too egotistical – to notice. That way we can sneak though on his blind side."

"Can I go back and try to locate Jack, before I met him I mean?" Lucie asked, emboldened by the recent praise from Scarlett. "Then I could warn him not to get involved."

"It would be great to tackle that one, Lucie," Scarlett said, sympathetically, "but I worry that it is far too close to Peter. The repercussions of altering that particular event would be huge. We need to think smaller I'm afraid and play the long game; look for containment at the very least. Maybe we could even use the portal to spy on them and see what they are planning. Let's just try something simple first, and see what happens. Has anyone got any ideas?"

"My brother lost his job a few weeks ago as part of this new financial system and he hasn't been able to find another one," said Andrea, one of Scarlett's old friends. "I couldn't help him in the Castle because all the light had gone. Let's see if we can do something for him. I propose going back before the light was gone, when things were still secure and people weren't worrying about the future and get him to protect his job somehow, with a more watertight contract. Then we will know if it has the potential to be successful and stand up to the darker powers that have taken over. If he still has a job next time we meet, we will know we can over-ride Nixon."

"That sounds good. All in agreement?" Scarlett asked. Everyone assented so they discussed how to proceed. The current lack of permanent contracts was making it much easier for bosses to get rid of their employees as the economic down turn meant that they could not afford to keep all the staff on. The country was on the verge of a financial meltdown and there was panic in the air. Andrea went through the portal, back to the Castle and visualised a permanent, legally binding contract for her brother. She was even able to go back and have a conversation with him in the past to encourage him to protect himself legally. He thought she was over-reacting, the country was booming, but she hoped the strength of the visualisations would work in her favour.

There was nothing more to be done. People went away from the meeting more hopeful than they had been on arrival. Now they had to wait to hear if Andrea's brother had his job back. It was also an opportunity to think of more ways to regain the lost ground.

Chapter 52: Small Signs

The new Inner Circle met at the same time the following day, back in Scarlett's office – which to all intents and purposes had become their new headquarters. Unfortunately, some of them – like Lucie, for instance – could not join them for every meeting because of the distance issue. Obviously, meeting at the Castle had made geography irrelevant, but now it was very much an issue as they could only convene in the natural realm – so as not to draw attention to themselves. There was nowhere in the environs of the Castle where it would have been safe for them to meet, so they just had to make the best of it. Fortunately, though, everyone who did live within easy reach of Scarlett's office was committed to finding a way to reverse what Nixon had done.

The news from Andrea was what they had all hoped for and it gave them a renewed sense of vigour. Her brother was working at his old firm as if nothing had happened in the mean time to interrupt that. A new history had been written for him, and although there were redundancies at his place of work, he was not one of them because his contract was water-tight. Andrea had spoken to him the previous evening and he had no recollection of the alternate course of time which had seen him lose his job. He did comment on the conversation they had had about his contract, saying that at the time he had felt she was overreacting and was inclined to ignore her suggestion because of the economic and workplace stability which existed, but that after their conversation, he had felt a strong compulsion – he called it a premonition, which made them all smile – to follow her advice and tighten up his contract. Others there had not been so fortunate, he had regaled her of stories about colleagues who had given years of service and lost their jobs because they were an easy target for the lawyers to find legal loopholes for.

Keeping with the plan that they had discussed the day before, everyone came to the meeting with someone in mind who they wanted to help. Seeing the success that Andrea had had, only served to encourage them further. They also discussed things which could be done to make small inroads in to the general trend Nixon had enforced of economic and financial turmoil, employment issues, insecurity, family break-down and social unrest. Many of the ideas which people had come along with were personal, to safeguard loved ones, but it was important they tried to impact national policy making and social issues as well, otherwise it would be like swatting flies while the lions ripped into the herd.

Rosie listened patiently to everyone talking – it was all very civilized, very 'British', as people took their turn to speak and listened with concentration and encouragement to one another. Eventually she felt the urge to share her own idea, as nobody else seemed to have come up with it. "I've been thinking about what Lucie said yesterday," she said, and people turned to face her, giving her their full attention. "I know we have to be careful who we approach so as not to raise suspicion, but why can't we go back to the Castle through the portal and target individuals from the Collective. We must all know people we have worked with in there, people we trust and believe in. Most of the children particularly who are still there are only going because they think Scarlett has endorsed it. We can try to talk to people we know locally face-to-face, but I think it would have more impact if we go back and warn them about what to look out for – otherwise we are in danger of just looking a bit paranoid. When you tell people what's wrong with the new system, it sounds like you're having a go at Nixon and Scarlett, because Shapeshifter has seen to that, but if people are pre-warned about what's going on they are probably more inclined to listen. That way, we can try to build up our numbers here – and maybe even gain spies within Nixon's ranks if anyone is willing to do that."

Xander sat forward in his chair, "I like that Rosie, what a great idea!"

"Well done Rosie, good thinking. Pick off his supporters one by one from right under his nose."

"This has to be done carefully," one of the adults urged, gravely, "and with people we know well and trust."

"Think of someone, people. No mistakes though, we have to stay under the radar with this," Scarlett urged them.

They spent the rest of the meeting taking it in turns to go back through the portal and tackle issues they had come with or go to the Castle in the past and try to alert people who they thought could be trusted to heed the warning. Spirits were rising and with it, hope.

Chapter 53: Phase Three

Nixon was riding high on his success. It had gone much more smoothly than he could have ever dared hope. He thought the young people would be more suspicious, less trusting of what he was trying to impose. But Scarlett had laid good ground work, they were used to operating in this realm and they liked to succeed. Their eyes had been lifted from the problems within society to finding solutions to those problems and they were still hungry for it. All Nixon was doing, as far as they could see, was to offer them a way that they could keep on doing that – and at a time when the needs were all the more obvious and the situations more extreme – and Scarlett herself (or so they thought) had blessed it. Shapeshifter would periodically make an appearance within the Castle as Scarlett, just to keep up the pretence.

The main difference, from the point of view of people participating in Nixon's version of the Collective, was that the guides were the ones providing the light for visualisations. They did not have a window to physically see the manifestation of their vision. They had to enter in to what Nixon termed a 'Partnership' with the guide and this would be the thing which facilitated the visualisation. Initially they were in control of the things they called for, but gradually – as with everything else he was connected to – Nixon changed the rules. It was very subtle, so as not to arouse suspicion, but basically the children were encouraged, more and more, to enter in to private sessions with their guide. This eliminated the possibility of a corporate response to something, or the chance for another person to alter the balance of things. Therefore, it was easier for the guides – as the relationships became stronger – to influence the course of events. Nixon, of course, was keen for his own plans to be progressed. His desire was for the nation to be dependent on him on as many levels as possible; for them to see him as the solution, the key to everything. He wanted power, worship, attention, control. As the balance shifted, the members were increasingly entering in to a trance like state – it was almost hypnotic on the part of the guides, drawing them in and misleading them, first by deceiving them about who or what these guides really were; then moving on to alter the perceptions of the children themselves about what they wanted to see change. The manipulation was such that the children were unaware of exactly what they had been party to, both in terms of their state of being and the things they had been led to focus on whilst they were in this state.

Moloch was delighted. The partnerships – because they were linked inextricably with his servants, the guides – had the effect of feeding his lust with almost the same amount of power as if they were actual sacrifices. To feed on someone's will and bend it or shape it as the guides did, was like devouring their very life force. By manipulating them in this way, they had taken over control of their very essence and identity. The more the children felt they were exercising their free will and entering in to a higher level of service to the Collective, ironically, the more they gave up of themselves. It was a tragic state of affairs which was so far away from the original vision. The Brightness was merely a servant, fuelling the ideas and the visions, but it had been supplanted and what nourished the visions now was about as far from light as you could get, yet it gave off the appearance of light. And nobody noticed!

After only a few weeks under his control, the Castle had become merely a place of passing through. It was a monument to the old way of doing things. The new doors had become a permanent feature and were now the destination as members would simply walk through them now, on arrival, entering into the dark corridors beyond. At the end of each corridor was a room – the antithesis of those which Scarlett had created. The stone walls were dark and cold; there was no natural light; there was no labyrinth – which itself had been the perfect symbol of collaboration and the collective mind. Instead, it was about the individual partnering with a single guide. It felt more secretive and hidden away and people began to respond to that, by themselves becoming more guarded and secretive. They operated alone and trusted nobody. It was now a place for single people to pursue individual agendas. Nixon was pleased with the transformation. Feeding this back in to the nation only served his purpose better – to separate and control. Add fear and paranoia to that and you could achieve just about anything.

Chapter 54: Freeing Captives

Xander was curious about what was going on in the Castle now, but he knew it would be dangerous to go there just to satisfy that. This was not a game, it was serious. He had seen the repercussions of what was going on in there affecting the people he knew. Lawlessness was becoming more common; rioting and looting; assault and robberies. He was confused by what Nixon was doing and wondered how having the country decline into anarchy was going to help him. It was frightening how quickly they had descended to this point. People were so fickle, he mused, going from the security and favour they had seen a few short months ago, to this and just accepting it as the norm. Why did they not long for the peace they had? Why not try to regain something of the atmosphere that had been lost? He was baffled by it. He could only assume that fear – which had been fed like a hungry fire – and hopelessness – a debilitating condition which robs you of all vision for the future – had come in and enslaved people, under the dark and festering leadership of Peter Nixon. People needed the gift of faith, that much was clear, but who was going to bring it, and where was it going to come from?

Xander had used the portal twice, once to help his dad and once to meet up with a school friend in the Castle. It stood in the corner of Scarlett's office, to the left of her desk, but it was not an imposing structure, it had a beautiful subtlety to it. It was a circular shape with three concentric circles making up its perimeter; each one moved in an opposite direction from the ones on either side of it. The wheels themselves were made of a bronze material, with teeth like the cogs of some giant clockwork machine on their outer edge. Between the rings was a narrow band of the most beautiful aquamarine. The centre looked invisible until you were really close to it. There you could detect virtually imperceptible tremors upon its surface – as though it were made of mercury or some other liquid that responded to the minutest of vibrations. As you walked through, there was the faintest resistance – as if you were walking through a high tension, microscopically thin skin. The closest thing he could equate it to was walking into a large spider's web – although it did not stick to you, at the critical point you just seemed to break through to the other side. Visualisation techniques were vital for this too, in order to accurately predict where you were to end up.

In response to Scarlett's appeal for help, he had thought it best to approach one of the other students from school. He had seen him around campus recently and he seemed to have quite a blank, vacant look about him, so Xander decided it was probably best to approach him in the past rather than try to tackle what was going on with him in the here and now. As Rosie had pointed out, when people were entrenched in the new regime, trying to point it out to them would look like paranoia – and maybe result in raising the alarm about what they were up to. He remembered having a conversation a while back with Nathan in the Community room, before all of this had kicked off. They had ended up collaborating over a visualisation for funding for the local playground. He had been able to use his journal to pinpoint the date which this had occurred on and used the information to go back to the Castle through the portal and wait for Nathan to emerge from it. Not knowing if he would literally bump in to himself there, he decided to wait outside the outer walls, but close enough to see clearly who was coming and going. There were no guides about at this stage – as far as he knew – as Lucie had told him the date of her first visitation from Naamah – but even so, Xander could not be sure that this was the case, or that Nixon was not able to track his presence there somehow, and it made him feel edgy to say the least. Eventually, Nathan emerged and Xander followed him towards the Elevator, tapping him on the shoulder when he was close enough.

"Nathan! Wait up!"

"Oh, Xander, what's the problem? Have you forgotten something?"

"No, mate, no. I just need to talk to you about something. Can we keep walking?"

"Yeah, I suppose. You can't talk to me about it back at school?"

"It's quite important, actually. I just wanted to say it now, while I saw you if that's okay."

"What is it?" He had picked up on Xander's tension and was looking intently at him.

"It's not easy to say. But seriously, you have to trust me on this. Can you do that?"

"Try me," Nathan challenged.

"Can you see those clouds?" he pointed up at a couple of innocuous fluffy white clouds that were barely noticeable.

"Yeah, what about them?"

"I want you to keep an eye on them. I know it sounds silly, because they just look like little clouds, but you'll start to notice them getting bigger, darker and more numerous. At some point not too far from now, the clouds are going to almost obscure the Castle completely and this will affect the Brightness."

"How do you know all this?" Nathan asked. But he didn't look sceptical, as Xander had feared. He had seen something in Xander's face and he believed him, however improbable it sounded.

"Just trust me on it, okay. When the Brightness is no longer able to carry our visualisations, you will be approached by guides – light people who look very beautiful and appealing – who will try to persuade you to go through new doorways. Don't do it. It's a plan to take over the Collective and control people. I know it sounds far fetched, but please, on no account go through those doors. Come and join us at Scarlett's office instead. We have set up a new Inner Circle there to try to correct things and we need people like you."

"I hear you. I'll watch out for what you've described and if it is as you say, well, then I guess I'll be seeing you at Scarlett's office instead."

"Don't talk to anyone about this conversation, just keep it to yourself. We can't risk a leak getting back to the wrong people."

"Who are the wrong people? Do I know who's behind this?"

"You do," Xander said, seriously. "Can I trust you Nath? I'm serious, you can't talk about this."

"I swear," Nathan nodded emphatically.

"It's Peter Nixon."

"No way!"

"Way! Look, I have to go. See you around. And thanks," Xander slapped his back before squeezing his shoulder, then visualised his return through the portal after he had watched the Elevator doors close on his newest ally.

When he arrived back in the office, a new member of the group sat there – Nathan. Xander smiled broadly at him, "Good to see you bud!"

Others had similar successes and their numbers did increase. But deep down, they all knew that this was never going to be the solution. It was only a matter of time before somebody rumbled them.

Chapter 55: Too Good to be True

Over the next few weeks, the portal was used successfully to go back to the Castle and warn people about the danger of the guides. There were also some successful trips back to alter the courses of events for family members and close friends. But it did not have the same scope as the Collective had done in its heyday, because only one person at a time could use it. Ironically, by changing the way the Castle itself operated – so that the children were forced to work one to one with the guides, Nixon had also imposed the same restrictions on them. His need for individual operators was all about control, theirs was certainly not by choice. However, they worked as effectively as they could under the conditions which had been prescribed for them. The other obvious and extremely confining factor, was that they were very conscious of not doing anything too radical because it was imperative that their actions remained, for as long as conceivably possible, under the radar. It seemed intolerable that the creator of the movement and some of its most successful members, should be reduced to what equated to a small, rebel satellite operation – and they felt the injustice of it keenly. But harbouring negative feelings was not a productive strategy; they would take what they could get, by force if necessary.

It was early May and they had been hiding out and covertly conducting business in the Collective to the best of their limited ability. The former Prime Minister had sadly died from the injuries inflicted upon him during the bombing, and his most loyal supporters – who had also been seriously maimed or mentally scarred by the events of that day – had made a quiet exit from politics. This left the way wide open for Peter Nixon. He had the remarkable ability – as most charismatics do – of charming and subduing even the most sceptical members of society. This was lethally combined with his hard line policies on anti-terrorism, social unrest and financial austerity, all of which were put in place to combat situations entirely of his own making. The initial rebelliousness and anti-social behaviour had calmed down to the point of an automaton-like acceptance (no doubt underpinned by his operatives heavily affecting the spiritual atmosphere over the nation.) With this, came a kind of heaviness. Although it was May, the spring had not really shown itself. Growth had been stunted and held back, the skies were brooding, battleship grey. People commented on it – try to stop the British talking about the weather! – but only a very few of them made the connection between what was going on in the Castle and the atmosphere over the nation.

By some absurd twist of fate, it was Scarlett who finally blew their cover. She had been avoiding the Castle so nobody would see her, but she had worked hard behind the scenes, strategizing with her team. She was in a meeting with Rosie, Dan and Xander – they had convened very regularly over the past few months, but exam time was nearly upon them, so the three of them were going to have to scale down their involvement for a few weeks. This meeting was a kind of debrief before their break. It was a positive atmosphere, in spite of everything, because they felt they were at least holding on to some ground.

"The portal is definitely working, it's given us that vital link with the realm of the Castle without having to come under Peter's filth," Xander spoke with vehemence as he uttered the last couple of words. "But is there anything else we can do? We are barely holding on to the ground we have, can we increase our position by, I don't know, making more portals? Something like that?"

"I've thought about it, Xander, believe me. I do nothing ***but*** think about it! But what worries me, is the more inroads we make into the realm there – through portals and such like – the more chance there is of us being detected. I'm amazed we've got away with it this long, to be frank. I thought Peter was more vigilant. I can only assume he feels he has produced something impenetrable – and I know that feeling, believe me. I fell into that trap myself. When you have finally made something you really believe in; when it seems to be working so well, just as you envisioned it, it's hard to comprehend something can go wrong. I was short-sighted, idealistic if you will, and I believed whole-heartedly in the Castle. You tried to warn me," she looked at Xander , who shook his head.

"Don't go there, Scarlett, it won't help."

"I know, but . . . well, maybe if I had listened, things would be different."

"You believed in your dream, there's nothing wrong with that," Rosie said, as ever the gentle encourager.

"There is when it blinds you to the truth. I will have to live with that mistake for the rest of my life."

"We learn to walk by falling down. The best thing you can do now is get up and come back stronger. Don't let him win!"

Just then, the phone on Scarlett's desk rang with the familiar internal ringtone to identify the fact that Jess was trying to get hold of her. A frown of impatience passed across Scarlett's brow. "I told her I didn't want to be disturbed," she grumbled, picking up the receiver. "Yes!"

A distorted version of Jess's voice was barely audible in the silence, as they all sat there watching Scarlett and waiting. Her expression changed from one of mild irritation to shock and horror. She replaced the receiver with a slightly shaking hand and got up.

"I have to go," she said, in a small, detached voice. "Sorry, we'll have to finish here."

"Scarlett? What is it?" Rosie asked, on behalf of them all, concerned for their mentor.

"It's my mum. She's collapsed and been taken in to hospital." She was pulling on her jacket as she spoke and heading towards the door. "Good luck with the exams and everything, see you soon."

"Scarlett?" Xander called after her, but she was gone.

Chapter 56: Below the Belt

Scarlett took a taxi to King's College Hospital, where her mum had been taken, and rushed in to the reception area.

"Good afternoon, madam," smiled a smartly dressed receptionist.

"My mother was brought in as an emergency patient. Harriet Tang. I don't know which ward she's on or anything."

"It's okay, don't worry, I'll just take a look on the system. Won't be a moment." She pecked away at the keys on her computer then looked up again, smiling. "She's been put on the David Marsden Ward, my love. It's on the third floor of the Ruskin Wing. Visiting time ends at 8pm. I can call up for you, see if she's taking visitors if you like?"

"I'm her daughter, I want to be with her," Scarlett replied, emotion thick in her voice.

"Very well. Go on up, they can tell you more on the ward."

Scarlett didn't hang around to make conversation, she headed for the lifts.

Two hours later, she left the hospital drained and dazed. Her mother had been fine one minute, according to eye witness accounts, doing a spot of shopping in Waitrose, when she had suddenly collapsed. She lay unconscious for some considerable time, coming round briefly in the ambulance but unable to communicate. She had returned to the comatose state and remained that way ever since. Doctors had examined her and scanned her brain, but could find nothing medically to account for her condition. Her father had turned up about half an hour ago and urged her to go home where he promised to contact her if there was any change. Reluctantly, she had gone. She found it hard to spend time in the same room as her father and she wanted to think about what was going on. It seemed to be suspicious to her that her mother would suddenly be struck down by something indefinable. By the time she had reached her home, she was both angry and convinced that someone – and no prizes for guessing who – had deliberately called this illness down on her mother to weaken her own position further and distract her from trying to involve herself in redeeming her vision. She wondered whether Nixon had something special planned and needed her out of the way. She immediately set about phoning members of her Inner Circle to share her theory. They assembled for an emergency meeting in her office. Some were initially sceptical, feeling she was being overly paranoid, but she managed to convince them that it was at least a possibility. Knowing how little Nixon valued life – and particularly anything associated with family – made it all the more probable. Dan offered to go and investigate – he knew a couple of people who were currently under Nixon's influence, but whom he hoped to be able to communicate with. Maybe there would be a rumour about what Nixon was doing to Scarlett or her family – particularly if he had phased her out and was leading it all by himself. It was worth a try and, reluctantly, Scarlett let him go.

It was about half past seven in the evening; Dan took the Elevator – something he hadn't done for months now – and loitered in the courtyard hoping to see his friend Oliver. He felt the cold, creeping fingertips of fear on his back and around his collar. He shivered. How could people keep coming and not see this place for what it was? He watched them as they entered the Castle Keep, completely oblivious to their surroundings, with almost a vacancy behind their eyes. How did it get to this? Suddenly Dan saw Oliver and caught his eye.

"Hey, Oli, How's it going man?"

"Cool. Haven't seen you around lately," Oliver looked at him suspiciously. "Where've you been?"

"Had a tough time at home, stuff going on, you know how it is. I'm here now though, committed to being here too."

"Glad you caught up, we need people like you." Oli seemed willing to forgive his recent lack of fidelity.

"Have you seen Scarlett around?" Dan asked, casually.

"Yes, she's up with Peter. They are running things together now, they make a great team."

So, as they suspected, Shapeshifter had continued his role as the anti-Scarlett, Dan thought to himself. If Oliver thought Scarlett was working with Nixon, he was never going to know of any plot to harm her or her family. It quickly became apparent that this line of questioning was not going to work.

"Coming in?" Oli asked.

"No mate, just leaving. Catch you soon though."

Again Oliver looked suspicious and Dan realised – as he walked away – that nobody else was going in his direction. In fact, an awful lot of people seemed to be coming in. It appeared that some kind of meeting had been called.

"Busted," Dan said, under his breath, as he increased his pace towards the Elevator. It had been a wasted journey, and probably a costly mistake.

Chapter 57: Seeing Double

Dan returned through the Elevator method to Scarlett's office – he had not needed to use the portal as he had been travelling in real time.

"Well?" asked Scarlett, hopefully.

His face said it all and a weight of anxiety and fear seemed to descend upon her. It was so hard to see her like this. Nixon had gone too far by making it this personal!

Dan told the group about his conversation with Oliver and what he suspected to be the implications of it.

"Oliver's probably talked to someone about you already. If they suspect you of some form of spying," Xander offered, "then they will feel it their duty to inform Nixon. It sounds as if he has the allegiance of everyone – particularly as he has Scarlett, apparently, going along with everything he says and does!"

"Which means I don't have long," Scarlett observed. "You said they were all going to some kind of meeting? We don't know if this is a regular gathering of the clan, so to speak, or a one off event with some twisted agenda. There are two options that I can see: option one, go in there with all guns blazing and challenge Nixon about my mother – hoping there are enough witnesses and that Shapeshifter is present so they realise there are two of me. This would have to be done before he has the time to realise that we are spying on him, otherwise we lose the advantage. I grant that it would be foolhardy, as we have no idea what he's up to or what kind of gathering he has called, or indeed, what power exactly he has at his disposal. I'd do it, don't get me wrong, although I'm just not sure of the merits of that plan." She paused, briefly, and nobody there doubted her bravery or her passion. "It would probably be a suicide mission and therefore of no value to my mother; or any of you." She looked around the room fondly at everyone who had stayed loyal to her. "I therefore propose option two," another pause as she collected her thoughts. Nobody dared to interrupt her, they waited expectantly for her plan. "I will use the portal to go back earlier today, before Dan met with Oliver so they are still not expecting anything. I will aim to find Nixon on his own, or without Shapeshifter, and I will approach him as that entity in order to ask questions about my mother. He hopefully won't suspect anything, he'll just think Shapeshifter is trying to assist him. What do you think?"

"It's a very risky plan Scarlett," Rosie ventured, looking worried. "What if you walk in on them and Shapeshifter is already there? How will you get out of that one?"

"Shapeshifter might know everything already, which will make it look suspicious if you go asking questions on his behalf," Dan added.

"Are you sure it's worth taking the risk, Scarlett?" Andrea asked, looking concerned for her friend.

"I have to know what he's doing to her!" Scarlett snapped back. "If it was your mother, any of you, wouldn't you do the same? If we know what he's doing we can either inform the doctors or tackle it here; take him on."

Nobody could argue with what she had just said.

"Okay then. Xander, can I borrow your hoodie? I don't want to be recognised until it's absolutely necessary." He took it off and handed it to her. Scarlett walked towards the portal and took a deep breath.

It was the first time Scarlett had been in to the Castle for weeks. Fortunately it was relatively quiet – due to the gathering that was scheduled for later in the day, most people, it seemed, had stayed away for now. Xander's hoodie covered most of her trademark red dress and she felt safe in her disguise. She took a gamble as to where Nixon might be, deciding to go to the Health room – as he was probably there working his evil magic against her mum, stirring his little pot of misery and disease.

To her knowledge, she was the only one in her rebel group to enter in through one of the new Castle doors – aside from Lucie, of course, who seemed to have been ***the*** first. It was just as she had described it;

colder, darker, greyer, uglier, with a faint whiff of sulphur. As she progressed along the corridor, she heard voices and hung back. Peter's voice was instantly recognisable.

"It is going to plan, Master. I have disabled Scarlett for the time being by striking her mother down. People are so weak when it comes to family members. She will not have the time or the energy to bother us. Shapeshifter is an excellent substitute and everyone has completely accepted him in her place. It adds that little bit of authenticity which people seem to crave."

"He is a good servant Peter, you have trained him well."

Who was that? Scarlett edged closer to the doorway, but nothing could have prepared her for what she saw next. A vast creature with the head of a calf and the body of a man sat on a throne, with his arms outstretched. She let out a tiny, involuntary gasp.

"What was that?" Moloch looked in her direction and the blackness of his eyes was deeply horrifying.

Thinking quickly, she ducked back to shake off the hoodie, then emerged in to the torch lit room.

"It is only me," she said, as boldly as she could. Trying to look like she had every right to be there.

"Shapeshifter?" Nixon asked, with just a hint of doubt in his voice.

"Yes, Master," she replied, trusting she had used the correct term of address – mimicking Nixon in fact – in the hope that she had fooled them. "How is the plan going to distract Scarlett? She's not likely to turn up later is she?"

"We will toy with her for a few days, I think; make her suffer a little. Her mother will not see out the month," Nixon declared, with glee, glad for the opportunity to boast of his prowess.

"How have you managed it, Master? What did you do?" Scarlett asked, trying to sound indifferent, but fighting hard to keep all traces of emotion out of her voice.

"What concern is it of yours?" Nixon asked, savagely. For a second, Scarlett worried that she had been rumbled, but he carried on. "Your job is not to ask questions, it is to serve us. You are nothing in this equation and you would do well to remember that. I can replace you at any time with someone whose allegiance is pure. Now leave us!"

Scarlett backed out of the room in a low bow. As soon as she could, she turned and fled – straight in to the path of her double.

Chapter 58: Dilemma

In the split second that it took to register her predicament, Scarlett had weighed up her options. They were: to allow herself to be captured and taken back to the room with Nixon and the beast in it – which she strongly felt she would not leave alive, as dramatic as that sounded – or to use the portal and betray their latest method of travelling in this realm, thereby rendering it useless from now on. Should she sacrifice herself for the others? It may keep them safe – for now – and give them a little more time with the portal, but they had all pretty much come to the conclusion that the portal was really only a temporary measure and was never going to be the solution. Or should she go? Go back to the others and dedicate herself, with them, to trying to find another resolution. There must be another way to defeat Nixon – there had to be! The alternative was just too horrendous to even consider.

Shapeshifter moved towards her with an unpleasant snarl on his lips – her lips, technically, which made it all the more unnerving. She hesitated for a second before summoning up the portal and jumping through it, feeling she had no choice, just as Shapeshifter lunged at her.

Chapter 59: Powerless

The portal had to be instantly dismantled, it was too dangerous to keep it. After the disastrous trip to the Castle, Scarlett was absent from the group for much of the time. Having failed to find the root cause of her mother's condition, she was unable to offer anything which could assist the doctors in their treatment of her. Scarlett had no choice but to wait at her bedside, knowing she had a maximum of about three weeks left to live – but Nixon could pull the plug at any time, so she was powerless to do anything. The doctors were kind and did all they could to make her mother comfortable, but at the end of the day, they had no clue as to what it was they were treating.

Eighteen months on from the beginning of this adventure, Xander looked round the red room at the people around him. What was it all about? What had it all been for? What should he do now? In Scarlett's honour, he gave himself two options: option one, walk away and probably never know the answer to his questions and watch Nixon take over completely, always wondering in the back of his mind if there was something he could have done; or, and he did favour this one slightly, option two, keep looking for the solution. They had been part of something amazing. Either the potential for that level of favour still existed somewhere, in some form or other, still waiting to be uncovered . . . . or the Collective had just been a good idea that had come and gone and the hope of something better was an empty promise.

Xander went for option two.

Available now . . . .

The Breakout

By Kate Pollard

Chapter 1: Forecast

"More of the same, I'm afraid," apologised Carol, the weather presenter - although it was hardly her fault. Xander roused himself and reached for the remote control to switch off another dismal forecast to round off another depressing day of news. His exams were over, it was past mid-June and he should be out enjoying his freedom with his mates. This should be the best summer of his life. Instead, he was sat indoors on a cold, grey, uncharacteristically poor - even for England - June morning. He felt as though the weather had permeated his skin and bone, turning him into a monochrome version of himself. It was as if a permanent lump of cold metal sat in his abdomen, occasionally pulsing out a frigid, acid wave through his core. How could he rouse himself? What should he do?

His thoughts turned to Scarlett whom he hadn't seen for several weeks now. He had heard from Jess, her secretary, that Scarlett's mother had passed away at the end of May and the helplessness and anger he had felt at the news welled up in him afresh. He reached for his phone and looked her up in his contacts as he had done numerous times before. He opened a text page and stared at it for a few moments before closing it again and throwing the phone petulantly in to the corner of the sofa where the arm met the seat.

"What's the use?" He spoke out loud, surprised by the sound of his own voice. Then he rose from the sofa and headed for the kitchen to perform his ritual cupboard opening performance.

Chapter 2: Grief

Scarlett looked across the shiny, marble top of the kitchen island in her parents' home at the man she hardly knew; her father. He had shrunk, physically it seemed, since the sudden loss of his wife. They had been doing this standoff dance for a couple of weeks and she was tired of it.

"What can I do, Dad?" she asked, shrugging and holding up her hands helplessly.

He looked up from the cup of tea he had been staring in to. "What?" he asked, vaguely.

"Talk to me!"

"Scarlett? Is that you Dear?" He didn't look at her, just through her, it seemed; in to the distant past where this pain was not even a fleeting thought.

Scarlett had to confess she was surprised by her father's reaction to his wife's death. She had always thought of him as a cold, unfeeling man. A part of her was angry with him for selfishly indulging in such emotions now. Why could he not have shown her mother this love while she was alive? Perhaps he had. She had to admit she didn't really know them, either of them, anymore. The Collective had been such a massive part of her life for the past few years that she had had little time for anything else. A pang of guilt accompanied this thought, along with regret.

She looked at the old man standing in the kitchen, once again staring in to his teacup. She wished he could be the strong, emotionally stunted man she had believed him to be right now, for it would certainly make this easier.

"What's the use?" she uttered, childishly, turning on her heel and walking out of the room; away from the claustrophobic hopelessness of grief and shattered dreams and out in to the cold, grey June day and a world she didn't recognise anymore.

Acknowledgements:

This book has been part of a journey lasting sixteen months, in which I wrote the sequel as well. It was as if The Brightness and The Breakout gradually revealed themselves to me chapter by chapter. The starting point was a combination of a dream I had a number of years ago relating to having twins, Perez and Zerah (see front quote) and a dream which my daughter had a couple of months before I started writing about a young woman leading children to find a saviour and in the process, their identities. I do not take the credit for imagining this story, it feels like a gift which I am deeply privileged to have been given.

On a personal note, I would like to thank my parents, Karen and David, for supporting and encouraging me throughout this process by reading and proof reading both manuscripts.

I would like to thank my daughter for the original seed of inspiration and for patiently listening to each chapter as it was written - both the first draft and subsequent ones.

Thank you to Rachel and The Big Blake Project for publishing the books for me and to Jane for being a sounding board for ideas. Thank you both for being the first to read the finished manuscripts and feed back to me.

Thank you to Martin Scott for years of inspirational input on turning a town, I have quoted some of your wise words!

Thank you, the reader, for purchasing this book and reading what I hope you will find an inspiring and engaging story about hope and possibility, destiny and love. Bless you.